M000191740

w/d
1-11-22

HOWARD STERN

HOWARD STERN

A Biography

Rich Mintzer

GREENWOOD BIOGRAPHIES

 GREENWOOD

AN IMPRINT OF ABC-CLIO, LLC
Santa Barbara, California • Denver, Colorado • Oxford, England

Copyright 2010 by Rich Mintzer

Library of Congress Cataloging-in-Publication Data

Mintzer, Richard.
    Howard Stern : a biography / Rich Mintzer.
        p. cm. – (Greenwood biographies)
    Includes bibliographical references and index.
    ISBN 978-0-313-38032-7 (hard copy : alk. paper) – ISBN 978-0-313-38033-4
(ebook) 1. Stern, Howard, 1954- 2. Radio broadcasters–United States–Biography.
I. Title.
    PN1991.4.S82M56   2010
    791.4402'8092–dc22
    [B]   2010000936

ISBN: 978-0-313-38032-7
EISBN: 978-0-313-38033-4

14 13 12 11 10   1 2 3 4 5

This book is also available on the World Wide Web as an eBook.
Visit www.abc-clio.com for details.

Greenwood
An Imprint of ABC-CLIO, LLC

ABC-CLIO, LLC
130 Cremona Drive, P.O. Box 1911
Santa Barbara, California 93116-1911

This book is printed on acid-free paper ∞

Manufactured in the United States of America

CONTENTS

Photo essay follows page 46

SERIES FOREWORD

In response to high school and public library needs, Greenwood developed this distinguished series of full-length biographies specifically for student use. Prepared by field experts and professionals, these engaging biographies are tailored for high school students who need challenging yet accessible biographies. Ideal for secondary-school assignments, the length, format, and subject areas are designed to meet educators' requirements and students' interests.

Greenwood offers an extensive selection of biographies spanning all curriculum-related subject areas, including social studies, the sciences, literature and the arts, history and politics, as well as popular culture, covering public figures and famous personalities from all time periods and backgrounds, both historic and contemporary, who have made an impact on American and/or world culture. Greenwood biographies were chosen based on comprehensive feedback from librarians and educators. Consideration was given to both curriculum relevance and inherent interest. The result is an intriguing mix of the well known and the unexpected, the saints and sinners from long-ago history and contemporary pop culture. Readers will find a wide array of subject choices from fascinating crime figures like Al Capone to inspiring pioneers like Margaret Mead, from the greatest minds of our time like Stephen Hawking to the most amazing success stories of our day like J.K. Rowling.

While the emphasis is on fact, not glorification, the books are meant to be fun to read. Each volume provides in-depth information about the subject's life from birth through childhood, the teen years, and adulthood. A thorough account relates family background and education, traces personal and professional influences, and explores struggles, accomplishments, and contributions. A timeline highlights the most significant life events against a historical perspective. Bibliographies supplement the reference value of each volume.

PREFACE

The First Amendment to the United States Constitution in the Bill of Rights states: "Congress shall make no law respecting an establishment of religion, or prohibiting the free exercise thereof; or abridging the freedom of speech, or of the press; or the right of the people peaceably to assemble, and to petition the Government for a redress of grievances."[1]

In the late 1950s, stand-up comic Lenny Bruce began his rise to stardom. A brilliantly clever comic, Bruce talked about social issues of the generation and the world as he saw it. However, unlike many of his peers, he was not shy about using obscenities in his comedy act. Bruce was not a joke teller but, instead, someone providing his own comedic views, in his own stream of consciousness style, which touched on all sorts of subjects in a free association rarely done successfully then or now. His comedy was heralded as genius by some, yet it was not appreciated or was easily dismissed by those who could not get past the somewhat uncouth manner of the presentation to digest the substance. It was indeed an example of judging a book by its cover.

Although speaking one's mind and even using expletives is much more acceptable in some cases today, especially on cable television channels, at the time such language was unheard of in many comedy clubs and public venues. As a result, Bruce was arrested at a performance in San Francisco in 1961 and charged with obscenity. Bruce was acquitted, but for the next few years he was frequently in trouble with the law for using obscene language on stage. In 1964, he was convicted on an obscenity charge in New York and spent a few months in jail. In spite of pressures, Bruce refused to clean up his language. "All my humor is based on destruction and despair," he said. "If the whole world were tranquil, I'd be standing in the breadline, right back of J. Edgar Hoover."[2] Little did Bruce know at the time, but he was changing the way entertainers would perform from that moment forward. His honest, no-holds-barred style influenced many well-known comedians such as Richard Pryor, George Carlin, Lewis Black, Eddie Murphy, and, although not a stand-up comic, Howard Stern. Lenny Bruce died of a drug overdose in 1966, but his legacy would remain forever. He was the groundbreaker who made it okay for performers to stand up for First Amendment rights and speak their mind, in their own words.

Bruce never received the attention or achieved the financial success of many of those who followed, especially Howard Stern. Bruce's career was constantly under scrutiny by those who sought to censor him at a time when testing the boundaries was unheard of. Although it is an often used cliché, to say Lenny Bruce was ahead of his time is appropriate. Had he been able to hear Howard Stern, he would be proud of what Stern has accomplished.

Of course others helped lay the groundwork for First Amendment rights for performers. The Smothers Brothers, who had a hit television show in the mid to late 1960s, were known as much for their battles with the television censors as for their comedy. Today Jay Leno and David Letterman make jokes about the president, the war, and other political issues nearly every night. Tom and Dick Smothers, however, received constant memos from CBS (the network that aired their weekly television comedy-variety show) informing them that they could not make jokes about the Vietnam War or the president or make any touchy political references.

The brothers continuously fought with the network, and their shows were constantly censored. Finally, the network dropped the series because the Smothers Brothers handed a show in too late to be edited (and censored), and the network claimed the episode "would be considered irreverent and offensive by a large segment of our audience."[3] The Smothers Brothers and the CBS Television Network ended up in court, and although the brothers continued to fight for their freedom of speech, they lost the case. They were offered a new series on ABC, but the series was eventually canceled in 1969. It is rumored that President Nixon was behind the cancellation of the program because he did not want comedy about his administration.[4]

AND THEN THERE'S HOWARD

Howard Stern took up the fight for freedom of speech when he entered radio in the early 1980s. Like Bruce and the Smothers Brothers, Stern would become the symbol of the next generation's fight against censorship. Of course this wasn't his intention, it just turned out that Stern had a dream of doing radio his way, and that meant stretching the boundaries of what was considered good taste.

Today, Howard Stern is the first name mentioned when nearly anyone is asked to name a radio personality. Yet Stern is not a hot up-and-comer, nor is he making headlines for his recent exploits. Stern embarked on a radio career three decades ago and remains at the top of his profession. His censorship battles with the Federal Communications Commission (FCC) are legendary and have been widely publicized. The fines he has generated from his on-air antics add up to more money than Lenny Bruce made in a lifetime of performing controversial comedy. Stern's free-spirited style is both loved and hated by millions. Even after being fired, Stern would always reappear somewhere else on the radio because he brought in huge sums of money to station owners wherever he went. Perhaps it has been capitalism that pushed what was and was not deemed respectable.

Howard Stern's story is one of being able to bring prurient interests, offbeat characters, and taboo topics to the mainstream. He has zig-zagged across the lines of good taste on numerous occasions, while broadening the scope of what may now be deemed acceptable on the airwaves. Like Bruce, the Smothers Brothers, and other First Amendment fighters who came before him, Stern will not back down if he believes he is right. Yes, Lenny Bruce would have been a big fan of Howard Stern, and Stern has always respected Bruce's work.

This biography of Howard Stern, the self-proclaimed "King of All Media," takes a look at Stern's career, from the pretend microphone in his parents' home to the very real multimillion dollar deal signed with Sirius Satellite Radio. Also covered is the world of Howard Stern, which includes his staff, the Wack Pack, the regular guests, and his wives, first wife Alison and current wife Beth, whom he married in 2008. Stern is at the center of a much larger universe than a radio program, with his own television network, two best-selling books, and much more. Does he deserve to make $100 million a year? Probably not. Nobody actually needs that kind of money. However, if anyone has put in long hours and tireless commitment to his craft, it has been

Howard Stern, who is relentless, and even obsessed, in his desire to give his fans the best programs possible day in and day out.

NOTES

1. Cornell University Law School Web site, United States Constitution, Bill of Rights, http://www.law.cornell.edu/constitution/constitution.billofrights.html.

2. John Michael Cohen, *The Essential Lenny Bruce* (New York: Ballantine Books, 1967).

3. Smothers Brothers Web site, www.smothersbrothers.com/smobro_bios/sb_bio_.html.

4. Steven Alan Carr, "On the Edge of Tastelessness: CBS, the Smothers Brothers and the Struggle for Control," *Cinema Journal* 31, no. 4 (Summer 1992): 3–24.

ACKNOWLEDGMENTS

I met Howard Stern several times at parties and other station events while working at WNBC radio in 1983. He was quiet, unassuming, approachable, and pleasant in our few brief conversations. Yet, listening to him on the radio, you would guess he might be a very different type of person. I have always admired the fact that he has a knack for keeping listeners at the edge of their seats. Sure, he can get a little over the top or gross sometimes, but he has certainly made radio far more interesting than anyone who came before or after him. Now, for $10 per month, I enjoy watching many of the great moments on Howard TV, not to mention great guests and lovely ladies. The shows are a diversion from the real world, and that's what Stern does best—enable his audience to step away from their troubles and concerns and into the world of Howard Stern.

Therefore, I thank Howard Stern for being a celebrity worth writing a book about. He has had an amazing career and continues to present new and entertaining material.

I also want to thank Bob DiForio for getting me this project; my editor George Butler; my wife Carol, also a fan of Stern who worked with him at a sleep-away camp many years ago; and my neighbor Michael C. Gwynne who had a small role in the film *Private Parts* and provided great insights into the moviemaking experience with Howard Stern. Also, thank you Doc (one of Howard's biggest fans), for pitching in.

INTRODUCTION

Howard Stern is among the most significant names in the history of radio. Since the early 1980s, he has built an immense following of dedicated listeners and fans while broadcasting from various radio stations throughout the country. He has also, through his desire to speak freely on questionable and often controversial topics, battled with censorship and has subsequently become a leader in the fight for freedom of speech.

Stern's goal, however, has not been to champion a cause as much as to provide original, edgy entertainment that pushes the limits of public acceptability. As a result, he has been at the center of controversy and debate over whether his brand of radio is decent or indecent.

Born on January 12, 1954, in Queens, New York, Howard Stern grew up insecure and with low self-esteem, but he also had the desire to make people laugh. Although his parents loved him very much, they were quite strict and did not always appreciate his sense of humor, which developed early in his life. His teenage years did little to bolster the self-confidence of the tall, gawky Stern, who was somewhat of an outcast, hanging out with a small group of friends that today would have been labeled "geeks." Although this was an uneventful time for the future king of radio, it did provide him with a great deal of material for his later years in media.

A good student in high school, Stern attended Boston University, where he briefly got his first taste of radio before being dropped from the college radio station for airing a taboo game show. It was also at Boston University that Stern would meet Alison Berns, who would later become his wife. Alison not only provided the support and encouragement Stern so badly needed but was also a frequent topic of his on-air banter, and she subsequently became a celebrity in her own right to Stern listeners. Together, Howard and Alison Stern would have three daughters, whom he loves dearly, though he always regretted not having more time for them because of the hectic hours required for his early morning radio shows. In fact, he would later acknowledge that his workaholic ways and ongoing desire to always create and produce the best shows possible were a large part of the ongoing problems in his personal life.

With Alison at his side, after college Stern embarked on a radio career that, like most DJs, would send him to various radio stations throughout the country. Little by little, while on the air in Hartford, Connecticut; Detroit, Michigan; and Washington, D.C., he would push to have more on-air time to talk and take phone calls from listeners rather than playing music. Wherever he went, the ratings for his time slots increased dramatically, bringing in more revenue to the radio stations. Station managers, although worried because they never knew what he would say or do next, encouraged Stern to keep doing his stream of consciousness brand of radio, even if the sexual references made them fear Federal Communications Commission (FCC) fines or sanctions.

Building a talented team as he went from station to station, Stern finally returned to New York City, and after constantly battling station owners at WNBC over the content of his program, he found a home with an FM rock station known as K-Rock. From there he emerged as the city's leading radio personality and in time become syndicated to markets nationwide. His no-holds-barred approach to radio content, including on-air games, off-beat guests, provocative interviews, and outrageous phone calls built a huge fan base while generating more fines from the FCC than any radio talent had ever amassed before.

Stern, however, was not alone in his mischief. His sidekick, Robin Quivers, along with comics Jackie Martling and Artie Lange, producer Gary Dell'Abate, sound engineer Fred Norris, and a host of other creative staffers all contributed heavily to the more than 20 hours of original content presented each week on *The Howard Stern Show*. Over the years, the staffers, the crew members, and even the odd characters making up what is called "the Wack Pack" gained notoriety on their own with articles, interviews, and Web sites posting their latest activities along with those of Howard Stern.

In the mid-1990s, Stern released two extremely successful books about his life. A movie would also be made in which he played himself.

The books and film received tremendous media attention, though critics and fans were divided on the assessment of the humor and the decency of the offerings. Nonetheless, Stern, who began billing himself as the King of All Media, had indeed broadened his horizons well beyond that of a radio star.

Radio, however, was still his bread and butter. It was where he had established himself as a household name. Stern talked about anything, especially taboo subjects. In addition, he presented a form of reality radio never before heard, with real stories from real people, often including strippers and porn actresses, many of whom were happy to disrobe for Stern and his staff. This added fuel to the censorship battles, and those who opposed what Stern was doing on radio were constantly writing letters to the FCC in hopes of driving him off the air. As a result, the controversy continued to enhance his image as a "shock jock." People tuned in to hear what Stern would do next, or how he would respond to the latest charges levied against him by the FCC.

Then, in 2004, Howard Stern became the highest-paid star in radio history. He signed a contract for half a billion dollars to join one of the two satellite radio networks that had just been launched. The massive amount of money, along with the opportunity to finally get away from the many censorship battles that ensued over the years on what was now being called "terrestrial radio," obviously attracted him. Stern became the face of the new form of radio and helped promote it to a higher level than ever anticipated, with millions of new subscribers. In addition, he also launched his own pay-per-view television network, HTV, where subscribers can watch his uncensored radio programs and become part of what has grown into a world of Howard Stern, with regular guests, frequent phone callers, a staff filled with comics, and a host of offbeat characters.

Stern, regularly heard daily on Sirius Satellite Radio, remains the leading force in radio today, and media pundits, entertainment reporters, and gossip columnists follow his latest activities. He has since been divorced from his first wife, Alison, and remarried. His second wedding, to model Beth Ostrosky, was a star-studded occasion that drew major media attention. Today, Stern remains one of the most notable, still controversial, highly paid superstars in the media. He still has his share of Stern-haters, but he has a large following who have learned that what he does on radio is one personality, but off the air he is a down-to-earth, caring individual who loves his wife and daughters, enjoys playing chess, and has a heart of gold.

TIMELINE: EVENTS IN THE LIFE OF HOWARD STERN

1954	Howard Stern is born on January 12.
1972–1976	Attends Boston University.
1978	Marries college sweetheart Alison Berns in June.
1978	Gets first morning show at WCCC-AM & FM in Hartford, Connecticut.
1982	Joins WNBC Radio in New York City.
1983	Daughter Emily Beth is born.
1986	Gets morning show at K-Rock in New York City.
1986	Daughter Debra Jennifer is born.
1986	*The Howard Stern Show* is syndicated to other markets around the country.
1988	First official FCC fines against *The Howard Stern Show* for $6,000.
1993	Daughter Ashley Jade is born.
1993	Releases autobiographical book *Private Parts*, which becomes an instant best seller.
1995	Releases second book, *Miss America*, which also becomes an instant bestseller.
1997	Appears in the film version of *Private Parts*.
1999	Announces that he and his wife Alison are separating.
2001	Divorced from Alison after 21 years of marriage.
2004	Signs $500 million deal with Sirius Satellite Radio in October.
2006	Starts on Sirius Satellite Radio.
2008	Marries Beth Ostrosky at star-studded wedding.

Chapter 1

THE EARLY YEARS

Howard Allan Stern was born on January 12, 1954, in Jackson Heights, Queens, a borough of New York City. Shortly thereafter, the Stern family moved to a hamlet in Long Island called Roosevelt, named for President Theodore Roosevelt. Stern's father, Ben, owned a recording studio in Manhattan, where Howard learned his way around a studio at a young age. His mother, Ray, was a homemaker for most of Howard's childhood. The second of two children, his sister Ellen is four years older, and today, although she is rarely ever mentioned on the radio program, he claims that they still have a good relationship.[1] "Stern describes his only sister Ellen, who is four years his senior, as 'completely opposite,' although they maintain a good relationship through their complementing personalities" (as quoted on http://www.answers. com/topic/howard-stern).

At an early age, Howard developed a love of comic books, which he started collecting. He particularly enjoyed those with superheroes, and Superman was his favorite. He also spent time pretending to talk into a microphone and playing DJ in his room. For Howard playing DJ meant more talking and less playing records, and he enjoyed the idea of trying to be funny and make people laugh from as far back as he or his family can remember. Although Howard claims his mom was too busy yelling at him and his dad was too busy telling him he was useless to recognize his genius, the young Stern was honing his comedic skills in private.

Howard's first attempts at being an actual showman were with his puppet shows starring Tito Stern. It was actually his mother's idea to get him interested in puppets. She thought playing with puppets would teach Howard to be more sensitive, a good idea that didn't quite materialize as Ray Stern hoped.

By the age of 12, Howard was doing puppet shows for a local senior citizens' home. Bored with the usual scripts, he would have his puppets simulate having sex. He claimed he wasn't trying to do anything tasteless, simply trying to keep the audience awake and make them laugh. Unfortunately, this cut short his nursing home entertainment days. However, he continued to perform even raunchier puppet shows for his friends. It was a sign of things to come in his career. "My parents weren't privy to the dirty performances, but my friends would beg me for puppet shows," recalled Stern in a 2003 *People* magazine interview. "I would have taken the whole stage and wrapped it around your head if I had known," was his father's response. "Imagine putting on a perverted puppet show in my basement."[2]

Howard has also claimed on the air that his parents were verbally abusive, and he has been quoted as saying that his mother ran the house with the intensity of Hitler. He also recalls that his father used to tape record conversations with Howard and his sister, asking them about items in the news. While his sister tried to answer with newsworthy responses, Howard was already quick with what his dad referred to as "wise guy" answers, so he'd tell Howard to "Shut up and sit down. Don't be stupid you moron." On his radio show, Stern later played some of these recordings to show the verbal abuse and used some of these old recordings in a commercial parody for the "Ben Stern School of Broadcasting," specializing in turning out self-loathing and emotionally disturbed workaholic media leaders. Of course, Stern also saw the warm and caring side of his parents, who were always supportive in his radio career endeavors. "I knew he always wanted to do something verbally," Ben Stern told a reporter for *Long Island Newsday* in 1993. "Anything he wanted to do creatively, I always supported him. I built him a stage for the marionettes. He wanted to have a band, so I got him a keyboard and wired it up and made him an amplifier," added the senior Stern.[3]

As he wrote in his autobiographical book *Private Parts*, Stern recalls that despite being a caring father, his dad could sometimes be unsupportive. "One day I made the mistake of saying to my father, 'Gee, I want to be on the radio. I'd like to be a millionaire.' He yelled, 'You idiot! You don't know anything about money! You never worked a day in your life!' But that's just his way of relating. I never felt unloved. I just felt like an idiot," wrote Stern.[4]

SCHOOL DAYS

Stern went from Washington-Rose Elementary School to Roosevelt Junior-Senior High School in the late 1960s. He was not very popular in high school and, in fact, as the neighborhood changed from predominantly white to much more African American, he was at the receiving end of racially motivated attacks because he was one of the white kids. In fact, even when Howard made some friends of color, they too would be beaten up just for being friends with him. While other kids enjoyed after-school sports, Howard's after-school activity was getting beaten up. As a result, he spent a lot of time indoors. When Howard was 15, the Stern family moved to Rockville Centre. "It wasn't any better in Rockville Centre," Howard later wrote in *Private Parts*. "I couldn't adjust at all. I was totally lost in a white community. I felt like Tarzan when they got him out of Africa and brought him back to England."[5]

Over six feet tall, thin, and gawky, the teenage Howard Stern spent most of his time hanging out at his friends' houses. Poker was among their favorite activities, and games would typically last for hours on a Saturday night. Other evenings were spent playing ping-pong or hitchhiking a few miles to go to movies, where, thanks to his height, Stern could easily pass for older than 15 and get himself and his buddies into R-rated movies. As for girls, neither Stern nor his friends were very popular and were considered geeks. Dating was not part of their social repertoire, and Stern was later quoted as saying to a reporter, "Girls never, never noticed me, and when they did, they noticed I was ugly."

In another interview, Howard explained, "Our rap was that if girls could only look beyond the fact that we didn't have great looks and seen that we had great personalities, they would have fallen in love with us. The truth of the matter was we had really bad personalities in addition to our ugly faces. Even the losers called us losers. And we were."[6] For Stern, the teen years were certainly nothing special—there was no hint of the stardom or adulation he would receive from both male and female fans in later years. The genius that lurked inside was quite well hidden during those post–puppet show/pre-radio years.

One summer, a teenage Stern served as a camp counselor at Camp Wel-Met in upstate New York. One female counselor who worked there at the same time recalls that Stern was "a tall goofy looking guy who was kind of quiet and hung out mostly with his friends. I only remember him now because he became so famous."[7]

Nonetheless, although his social life was not very exciting, Howard did well in school. He did not devote a great deal of time to school work, but he was smart and able to catch on quickly, which resulted in good grades. He once claimed on air that English was his favorite subject.

Stern remained focused on his interests, which included broadcasting, movies, and the media. He used his video camera on occasion to make films with his friends. Stern also learned to play chess during his teen years (according to his father, the boy who first taught him to play was not very good at it), something he would enjoy over the years and become enamored with as an adult. For Stern, it was his foibles, his insecurities, and his years spent as a geek that would eventually translate into very real, very funny on-air stories. He used these very real stories to establish himself as vulnerable and relatable, ultimately drawing numerous listeners who could relate to being picked on, left out, and rejected during their own awkward teenage years.

Not unlike the neurotic humor of Woody Allen, Rodney Dangerfield, and many other great comics, Stern tapped into his own vulnerability for comic purposes, making fun of his own lot in life. Had he been very handsome, popular, and a high school quarterback, Howard Stern might never have had the material to draw from and attract such a massive audience of dedicated listeners.

BOSTON UNIVERSITY

Stern went to Boston University, a school of 30,000 students and 4,000 faculty members that was larger than the entire town of Rockville Centre. Although Stern is among the most controversial notables to attend the university, he is on a long list of famous alumni that includes Martin Luther King Jr.; attorney F. Lee Bailey; Tipper Gore; Bill O'Reilly, host of the news program *The O'Reilly Factor*; actor Paul Michael Glaser; and actresses Geena Davis and Marisa Tomei. A regular guest on the Stern show, comic Greg Fitzsimons also attended Boston University.

Stern gained his first radio experience at the college radio station, WTBU, and first tested the waters of controversial broadcasting, creating a comedy game show called "Name That Sin," in which students confessed their worst sins. The show was canceled after the first broadcast: Stern had officially experienced his first battle with on-air censorship—and lost.

Despite the fact that Stern graduated with a 3.8 grade point average, and now quietly provides money for a scholarship to Boston University, some of the school officials don't seem to want to recognize that the "shock jock," as he's often been called, attended their esteemed school. Alumni and radio producer Tom Somach, upon attending his 25th college reunion at Boston University's College of Communication, commented that the school's Wall of Fame displayed photos of Pulitzer Prize–winning *New York Times* reporter Don van Natta Jr., Fox News host Bill O'Reilly, former ABC executive Ted Harbert, and CNN reporter Gary Tuchman. Conspicuously missing was any mention of Howard Stern, who has likely passed all of the others in wealth and overall notoriety, for better and for worse. "BU is embarrassed by any public connection to Stern. They won't even acknowledge his existence," says Somach.[8]

Although Boston University may not want to recognize Stern, he owes them a debt of gratitude, not only for giving him his first taste of radio and censorship but also for accepting a young student named Alison Berns. Alison, a year younger than Howard, was studying to be a social worker and would later get her master's degree in social work from Columbia University in New York City. Alison was much like Howard, in that they were both somewhat withdrawn and preferred to blend into the crowd rather than draw attention to themselves. They were immediately drawn to one another.

In a 1993 interview with television talk show host Charlie Rose, Stern talked about meeting Alison. "I could not believe when I met Alison, that she would be interested in me. I know I'm not a handsome man and certainly shy and awkward with women, and the idea that this normal and beautiful woman—up until that point whenever I dated, (it was usually) some freaky women, let's put it that way—suddenly she's not only paying attention to me but wants to spend the rest of her life with me. I think it was because I could make her laugh," explained Stern of Alison's interest in him."[9]

Initially, Stern, who had taken an interest in transcendental meditation, asked Alison to be in a film he was making on the subject. He had been dabbling in film making since his high school days and used it as a means of displaying his creativity. It was also a way to meet women. Of course, it never worked in that respect until Alison came along and was more interested in spending time with Stern than actually being in the film. Nonetheless, Alison agreed to be a part of the film, after which Stern asked her out. Their first date was, appropriately enough, to see the film *Lenny*, based on the life story of Lenny Bruce, who would have a strong influence on Stern's career.

From that point forward Alison became a significant part of Howard Stern's life, sharing in his world while also being very supportive.

Alison was Stern's first real girlfriend, and he cherished their time to-gether. They shared an offbeat sense of humor and came from similar backgrounds. Like Stern, Alison was Jewish, although over the years Stern's Jewishness has come into question many times—mostly from his claims of being half Jewish and half Italian. Stern worries about anti-Semitism and has been quoted as saying his half Jewish side has been beaten with chains. The truth is that both of his parents are Jewish. Stern's Hebrew name is *Tzvi*, and his paternal grandparents, Froim and Anna (Gallar) Stern, and maternal grandparents, Sol and Esther (Reich) Schiffman, were all Jews who immigrated to America at about the same time.[10]

DOING THE UNTHINKABLE

After graduating magna cum laude, Stern, despite his passion for radio, did the unthinkable. In 1976, he took a job in advertising at Benton and Bowles, a major advertising agency in Manhattan. Stern was worried that a career as a DJ would not allow him to support a family. When speaking more seriously during interviews, Stern often acknowledged that his father also worried that Stern would have a hard time in the rough radio business and would not make much money. Stern's dad had seen a lot of radio people in his days as an owner of a recording studio. Radio traditionally did not pay very well unless you were a top celebrity, and Stern knew this. That, coupled with his desire to make his father proud, led him to initially opt for advertising over radio.[11] Had Stern stayed with advertising, one can only dare to imagine some of the television commercials he would have tried to put on the air.

Stern was also concerned about the lifestyle of a radio DJ, which meant going from low-paying job to low-paying job at small radio sta-tions around the country to build up a career. This might entail over-night timeslots, weekends doing promotional activities for the station, and so on. He knew it could take a long time to make any real money in radio and feared Alison might not want to follow his dream while crisscrossing the country and getting by on a meager income. She had a degree in social work and wanted to pursue that as a career.

Although advertising work may appear to be a creative endeavor, it is also largely about pleasing a client, even if the client's ideas are not very clever. Stern, to this day, has never been a very big fan of appeasing someone else if it means stifling his own creativity and self-expression. As a result, he hated the job. Nonetheless, he stayed because he thought it was the more responsible thing to do and a potentially more stable career choice. But both Alison and his mother convinced Stern to follow his dreams of a radio career and quit the advertising job. From that point forward, Alison played a major role in Stern's success by providing the support and confidence he needed. She believed in him from the beginning. Stern later acknowledged Alison's role in his foray into radio and how she stuck by him through the lean times by dedicating the film *Private Parts* to her.

On June 4, 1978, Alison Berns and Howard Stern were married at the reformed Temple Ohabei Shalom in Brookline, Massachusetts, in a small ceremony attended by their families and close friends.

ENTERING RADIO

Stern started in radio, while still in college and rather unceremoniously, in 1975, as a DJ at several small radio stations that featured mostly disco music—WNTN in Newton, Massachusetts, then briefly after college at WRNW in Briarcliff Manor, a small town in Westchester, New York (before the brief advertising stint mentioned above). Stern would later serve briefly as program director for WRNW in 1976, but it was not the behind-the-scenes activities that drew him into radio or particularly interested him. He later made it clear in many interviews that he could never have lasted as someone simply playing songs; he needed to do more. Stern contended that anyone could spin records, but it took a lot more creativity to get behind the microphone and actually entertain your audience.

In 1978, Stern landed at a rock station in Hartford, Connecticut, WCCC-AM and WCCC-FM, where he was given the important morning drive-time slot. This was the period in which radio drew its largest audience: listeners getting ready for work or driving to work. Many of the listeners tuned in largely for the news, weather, and traffic reports, but some DJs were already trying their hand at bringing comedy to their programs, typically in quick bits, or jokes, in-between records.

At the Hartford station, Stern was in his element, playing mostly hard rock, of which he was a fan. But his goal was to play less music, and this job gave him the opportunity to talk to commuters on their way to work and the many people who felt compelled to call a radio station. Station owner Sy Dresner encouraged Stern to start taking phone calls, and slowly but surely, Stern started to banter with callers on air and work some of his own stream of consciousness and off-the-cuff humor into the daily morning show. Clearly, the results were positive as phone calls increased and the ratings were very good.

Radio was, and still is, all about ratings, which provide information on who is listening and when. Ratings are broken down into demographics, or statistics about the listening audience, including age group, gender, lifestyle, and income. Advertisers use the demographics to try to reach a specific audience. For example, if you make a product that you want to sell to 24-year-old men who make over $30,000 a year, but are still living at home with their parents, advertisers can zero in on this market.

MEETING FRED NORRIS

During his time at WCCC, Howard Stern not only honed his talk show skills but also met Fred Norris, who has worked with Stern ever since as a sound producer and writer. When they met, Norris was the late night DJ. A year younger than Stern, Norris, who had changed his name from Nukis, was known for his intellect. In fact, after skipping fifth grade, Norris and a fellow student went on to win a middle-school science fair by creating an amplifier that could be worn on the arm, allowing the wearer to hear his or her own heartbeat without a stethoscope. Norris and his partner made the front page of the local newspaper for their efforts.

Norris and Stern shared a desire to make it as DJs. Like Stern, Norris was rather quiet and unassuming off the air. However, he did not possess Stern's unique ability to take on a new persona behind the microphone and stand out from the many DJs trying to make it to the major markets, like New York, Chicago, and Los Angeles. The friendship proved quite fortuitous for Norris as it has provided steady work and high pay in an industry that is anything but stable. But it was more than friendship that brought Norris into the world of Howard Stern. Norris was a jack of all trades—a musician, radio producer, writer, and entertainer in his own right. He provided Stern's shows with creative ideas plus impressions of a slew of celebrities ranging from Bill Clinton, Jack Nicholson, and Mick Jagger to Stern's father, and fellow staffers Artie Lange, Robin Quivers, and others.

Years later, Norris met his wife, also named Alison, on a dial-a-date segment of the show. In addition, a popular game show segment, "Win Fred's Money," became an ongoing favorite of *The Howard Stern Show*. A trivia contest, the objective is to see whether Norris or a guest listener can correctly answer more trivia questions in a rapid-fire format. The winner can potentially walk away with $5,000. Norris, however, never ceases to amaze, and wins almost every time. Audiences appreciate Norris's uncanny ability because the loser's wife or girlfriend (or the loser herself) has to strip naked in the studio while the show is on the air. This later gained greater significance when the show began being taped for television.

MAKING THE HEADLINES

Stern made a name for himself while in Hartford. In 1980, former Beatle Paul McCartney, who appeared on the Stern show a number of times in later years, was arrested while on tour for possession of marijuana. On air, Stern made a long distance call to Japanese government officials in an attempt to get McCartney out of jail. His efforts failed, but his popularity grew. Yet, despite his growing popularity and the increased ratings for the station during the morning drive hours, Stern left WCCC in 1980 over a contract dispute: the station owner refused to give him a mere $25 a week raise. Stern was not worried about finding another job, however. His style was drawing attention, not only from listeners but also from station managers and owners.

TO DETROIT, WASHINGTON, AND BEYOND!

Stern answered an ad for a morning radio personality at a rock station in Detroit, WWWW. For a salary of $30,000, Stern became the morning voice of "the 4W" in the Motor City.

Stern had ongoing, yet mild, battles with the station manager in his efforts to talk more and play less music. Nonetheless, he was able to work his brand of morning radio onto the airwaves between songs, and for his efforts he won local DJ awards. He took phone calls and did offbeat interviews, including those with prostitutes, which kept listeners glued to a new brand of talk radio.

Unknown to Stern, however, the Shamrock Broadcasting Network, which had purchased the station shortly before Stern arrived, had other plans for their future. The network officials concluded that the very urban, northern city of Detroit had plenty of rock stations, but no country music stations—and after all, wasn't Detroit just a stone's throw away from Nashville and Graceland? Okay, a very long stone's throw. Nevertheless, the owners made the switch and featured Stern as "Hopalong Howie." Shortly after the decision to go country, Howie decided to hopalong right out of there. In his 1994 film *Private Parts*, Stern does a scene in which he stops a country song midway through, claims he doesn't understand country music, and quits his job.

Picking up and moving yet again was not easy for Howard or Alison, but it is part of the life of a radio personality. Fortunately for Stern, his uncanny ability to raise the ratings in the always competitive morning drive time slot once again brought him plenty of attention from station owners and managers, and he opted for station WWDC, in Washington, D.C.

One of the most important factors for Stern in choosing a station and a market in which to be heard was moving forward in his career. Sure, other radio DJs talked with listeners and guests, but they were typically formula interviews or scripted conversations. Stern was already looking for unusual topics people did not typically hear on the radio. He didn't want to be just another DJ and had already set himself apart from the crowd. By 1981, when he talked to the station owners in Washington, D.C., he knew he wanted freedom to talk, play fewer songs, and become the number one radio show in the city. He did not mention that his plan was to use Washington as a stepping stone back to his hometown, New York City, the number one market in the country. While working out the details of his contract, Stern had a couple of requests. First, he wanted to bring in Fred Norris, whom he hadn't worked with since his days in Hartford. The two had remained friends and Stern knew Norris was a good producer. He also wanted a sidekick, someone he could play off and who could respond to his ongoing stream of consciousness.

The closest the station let him get to having a sidekick was to have his own newsperson read the top news stories on the hour. Station manager Denise Oliver gave him a tape of a woman newscaster named Robin Quivers and gave Quivers a tape of Stern from his days in Detroit. It was a good match and both agreed to try it out. The station, however, thought it was unprofessional for Stern to talk to the newscaster during the show. Little did they know that Robin Quivers and Howard Stern would emerge as the preeminent team in the modern era of radio. Sure, Stern was still the star, but Quivers would play a significant role in the future of the show and in Stern's life.

MEETING ROBIN QUIVERS

Now that Stern had gained confidence, proving himself as an up-and-coming force to be reckoned with in radio, Alison could relinquish her role as the woman behind the man and turn it over to Quivers. In the case of the self-proclaimed "King of All Media," as Stern later billed himself, Robin Quivers was in essence his queen, at least professionally speaking.

An unlikely pairing, Stern and Quivers teamed up in Washington, where despite the station repeatedly warning Stern not to talk to the newscaster, he continued to bounce ideas off Quivers and ask for her opinions. She often played the role of straight woman to his comedy. That was how Robin Quivers learned the role of sidekick, while on air and often without warning, as Stern would extemporaneously involve her in whatever he was up to.

Quivers had no real comedic training and was not expected to bring comedy to the show. However, she responded to the political, social, and personal matters Stern dangled in front of listeners to keep them entertained. Not only did it work on air, with Quivers's infectious laugh serving as a genuine laugh track, but over time they gained a tremendous professional respect for one another that has kept them together for nearly 30 years. In fact, when Quivers has to miss a show, Stern rarely goes on without her, opting instead to air a rerun in her absence.

ABOUT ROBIN QUIVERS

A biography of Howard Stern isn't complete without getting to know his partner. Robin Quivers hails from Baltimore, Maryland. Neither of her parents had more than a seventh-grade education, and the family had little money. As she later described in her autobiography, *Robin Quivers, A Life*, she was sexually molested by her father. Recognizing how far she has come after such a painful childhood, Robin Quivers works today with charities that help children who have been sexually molested.

Needing to get away from her family life, Quivers joined the United States Air Force where she served as a nurse and reached the rank of captain. After her stint in the military, she went to the Broadcasting Institute of Maryland. After graduation she found a job at DC101, shortly before Howard Stern joined the station. Smart, outspoken, occasionally temperamental, but always at Howard's side, Quivers has developed her own loyal following who appreciate her as a woman with conviction in a very male-dominated industry and on a very male-oriented staff. She is usually the lone female voice on *The Howard Stern Show*, unless a female guest is also on.

As an African American woman, Quivers has been criticized for working with Stern, given that he makes his share of racist jokes and comments and his show exploits women as sex objects. So, why did Quivers stick with Howard Stern? Largely because she met him off air and soon realized that it's all part of the show, a show based on reality but designed to grab attention using any method available, even offensive humor. Like Alison, Quivers caught on very early that there is a distinct difference between the Howard Stern on the radio and the one who in real life is reserved, often uncomfortable around people, and respectful and loyal to the people he cares about. Quivers has always seen the vulnerability behind the voice and knows the real Howard Stern.

In her radio development with Howard Stern, Quivers also learned, despite very candid on-air conversations about her real life, that on-air and off-air personas can be very different. As she once told a reporter in an interview, "You are always giving a performance when you're on the radio. I don't come on and do whatever I feel like doing. I do 'me' for the show."[12] Apparently it has worked very well, as she is among the most well-known personalities in the industry and has been approached by radio and television producers to do her own talk show, although such a project has never materialized.

Quivers appreciates the humor of the show even when it is sometimes aimed at minorities. Whether they are talking to a rock star or the foul-mouthed, belligerent Yucko the Clown, a regular guest of the show, they are trying to entertain a listening audience that is wondering what they will hear next. Stern also knows that despite their occasional on-air battles, Quivers understands their brand of humor, which is why she has also backed him 100 percent when station managers, the Federal Communications Commission (FCC), and others give them a hard time about the content of the show.

LEAVING DC

It didn't take long for Stern to achieve his goal of topping the Washington, D.C., morning drive competition. He talked quite openly and candidly about his own personal life, sometimes crossing the line and being chastised by station management. Other times, he simply went too far. A scene in the movie *Private Parts* recounts Stern talking about Alison's miscarriage on the air. She had become accustomed to his frank openness about their life together, though she occasionally had to reel him in a bit. The scene concludes with Stern going to commercial, and the look on his face shows that he realizes that he has gone too far. Although Stern was always ready to do battle with station owners and managers and had little respect for the FCC, which he felt clamped down on his first amendment rights, he never wanted Alison to feel like a target of his attacks. In time they got past this difficult episode.

During his two-year stint in the nation's capitol, Stern not only found the perfect foil for his humor, but he also established himself as a dangerous force to be reckoned with in the radio community. Off-beat on-air games and sketches were sprinkled into the banter, and Stern had a way of holding the attention of his audience who couldn't turn him off, not wanting to miss whatever was coming up next.

Station managers around the country courted Stern though they knew he would be a challenge with his controversial style that often rattled sponsors, drew flack from various women's and religious groups, and was becoming a thorn in the side of the FCC. At the same time they knew he could put a station on the map, and their ratings and revenue would grow quickly.

Then, January 13, 1982, a blizzard hit the Washington, D.C., area. Schools were closed, as was National Airport for a time. Among the many delayed flights was Air Florida's Flight 90 from D.C. to Fort Lauderdale. When the plane was finally cleared for take off at 4 P.M., it went down the runway but never really got off the ground, crashing into the 14th Street bridge, which had a significant amount of traffic on it at that time. Five people on the bridge were killed as the plane sent drivers into the icy waters. The plane crashed into the water, killing all but five of the more than 70 people on board.[13]

Although acknowledging that this was a terrible tragedy, Stern later made a mock phone call to Air Florida asking if the 14th Street Bridge would now be a regular stop. Station owners and sponsors were not amused, and many listeners thought Stern had crossed the line. He later commented that his intention was to show the airline's incompetence for allowing something terrible like this to happen. Although Stern remained with the station for a few more months, this well-publicized incident was the end of his days in Washington, D.C., and led to the firing of both Stern and Quivers.

WELCOME TO THE BIG APPLE

The next stop for Howard Stern, Robin Quivers, and Fred Norris was WNBC, one of the most powerful stations on the AM dial in New York City. Stern had made it full circle back to New York City, the largest radio market, and where he had hoped to end up all along. Little did the executives at NBC know that this would become a far more challenging and confrontational relationship than they had ever imagined.

Stern joined WNBC in 1982 and began broadcasting from the NBC studios on the second floor of the famous 30 Rock building, the hub of Rockefeller Center, a popular tourist attraction. The building has been the home of many television and radio programs over the years, including David Letterman's late night talk show, several stories above. Stern's glass-enclosed studio was typically a viewing stop for the ongoing tours of the famous facility, where visitors would watch whichever DJ was on air for a few minutes.

Unlike his previous stops, Stern was not given the morning show, but instead an afternoon time slot. The morning belonged to the very popular Don Imus, who had already been with the station for several years. The *Imus in the Morning* program was the highest billed morning show in the New York market. Like Stern, Imus pushed the limits on what was acceptable. He did a number of characters, mocking evangelists, politicians, and other notable figures. He was quick to attack those he did not like. Clearly, the station saw the immense possibilities of marketing their two celebrity on-air talents together and featured television and print ads that read "If We Weren't So Bad, We Wouldn't Be That Good." Although the two appeared on many billboards together and at many promotional events, Stern and Don Imus were never more than working partners at the radio station.

They were both billed as shock jocks for being outspoken and voicing their opinions on the air. Imus, however, was more focused on the politics and people making the news. He had an ax to grind. Stern took a different approach. While also talking openly about celebrities, he preferred exploring more prurient interests and had a greater focus on sexuality, lesbianism, offbeat characters, and off-color humor.

Both had very large followings, but there was a very distinct difference in their bad boy images. Perhaps the biggest on-air difference was Stern's vulnerability versus Don Imus's arrogance. An even more telling sign was their off-the-air personalities. Stern left his raunchy, unabashed radio persona in the studio and remained reclusive. He was respectful to most of the people he met and openly talked about his goal of being the best radio personality in New York, but beyond that he had no other agenda. In contrast, Imus became known as the same cantankerous, angry personality off air as he was on air—sometimes even worse. In time, the two grew to loathe each other.

In a 1984 interview, Imus was quoted as saying "Howard's a slut too, plus a Jew bastard, and should be castrated." Stern played a clip of this interview in the news section of his November 5, 2007,[14] show when Imus was in the news as part of a major controversy regarding one of his racist comments about the African American athletes on the Rutgers women's basketball team. A later comment about Pacman Jones, an African American football player, also drew similar criticism. During an on-air conversation about the arrests of suspended Dallas Cowboys cornerback Adam Jones, Imus asked, "What color is he?" Told by sports announcer Warner Wolf that Jones is African American, Imus responded, "There you go. Now we know." Imus later said the comment was misunderstood, but his explanations fell mostly on deaf ears.[15] At other times, on the rare occasion Stern and Imus were in the same place at the same time, they would get into name-calling shouting matches.

As for Stern's approach to radio at WNBC, anyone listening back in 1982 would agree that he was being very real, open, and honest about himself. He talked about his wife Alison, their personal life and sex life, and anything else that came into his stream of consciousness.

As illustrated in the movie *Private Parts*, not long after starting at the station, despite promoting him as a bad guy, station management and Stern frequently held pre-show meetings to discuss what he had done on the air the day before. They wanted Stern to be bad, but not really bad. Station manager John Hayes, whom Stern nicknamed "Pig Vomit," was perhaps missing the point that pushing the boundaries was why so many listeners tuned in to hear what Stern had to say. There was a lot of disagreement about what was and was not permissible on radio. Much of what Stern did had never been done before, and, back in 1983, no clear-cut rules were in place. Stern backed up his argument with two valid points. First, there was freedom of speech as supported by the First Amendment to the United States Constitution. Second, he was getting the highest ratings in the city during his afternoon time slot, which meant more revenue for the station.

At WNBC, Stern tried out new game shows, made prank phone calls, took listener phone calls, asked personal questions, and even put out the first invitation for a woman to come into the studio and strip during his show. Convinced that this would happen, Stern kept promoting that he would have a naked woman in the studio. Unfortunately, no one came in to fulfill his wishes. So, after nearly a week of seeking his first on-air stripper, Stern, knowing his popularity, decided to punish his listeners. For the next week Stern did nothing but play an ongoing string of what he considered to be the worst tunes he could dig up while basically taking away the comedic antics that made the show such a hit.

The NBC executives did not know what to make of it, because Stern was technically doing nothing wrong. In fact, he was, for a change, following the playlist, while adding what he considered bad pop music. Finally, after a week, his fans could no longer stand it. The glass viewing windows were covered with brown paper, and a couple of listeners hired strip-o-gram strippers to show up at the NBC studio and disrobe. This was the introduction of strippers on *The Howard Stern Show*.

GARY DELL'ABATE (BABA BOOEY)

At WNBC Stern also met Gary Dell'Abate, who was called on to produce the show. Born into a large Italian family, 12 children to be exact, Dell'Abate had a fraternal twin brother who died shortly after birth. Like Stern, Dell'Abate had grown up on Long Island. However, unlike Stern, he was very popular in high school and active in school activities, including the astronomy club, the wrestling team, the school newspaper, and the radio station where he served as a DJ. He attended Adelphi University where he interned at several college radio stations and finally at WNBC.

Today, Dell'Abate is still with *The Howard Stern Show*, largely because he is an excellent producer, providing the organization and attention to detail Stern needs. He also has a strong work ethic and incredible dedication to the show and his job. As producer, he screens and books guests, schedules interviews, puts together show segments, makes sure everyone is on the same page for the broadcast, and then reviews what did and did not go well afterward. Dell'Abate keeps files on guests, frequent callers, and a variety of offbeat characters known as "Wack Packers." He manages all aspects of what is probably the busiest radio show on earth. Most significantly, Stern has trust and tremendous confidence in Dell'Abate, which frees him up to do his thing, the creative and entertainment portion of the program.

Very prominent teeth and big lips have made Gary Dell'Abate the butt of many on-air jokes, which may be inevitable when dealing with Howard Stern, Robin Quivers, Jackie Martling, Artie Lange, and a host of staffers and off-beat guests, all of whom are trying to be funny. Generally, Dell'Abate takes it all in stride, confident in his status as the guy who maintains order in what might otherwise be considered the chaotic world of Howard Stern.

His nickname, BaBa Booey, comes from his mispronunciation of a character in the old Quick Draw McGraw cartoons named Baba Looey. Dell'Abate has established himself as arguably the most well-known producer in radio. However, like Stern, he also takes an unassuming role while he is away from the show, living in a wealthy neighborhood in Connecticut and spending time with his wife and sons.

IMPORTANT STERN EVENTS

In the early 1980s, two very significant events took place outside the radio studio for Howard Stern. In his personal life, Howard and Alison had the first of their three daughters, Emily, who was born in 1983. Then, in his professional life, Stern appeared on David Letterman's late night program in June 1984 and became known at a national level. Letterman was a fan of Stern, and it would be the first of many more appearances on the famed late night television talk show.

In early 1986, Stern was fired from WNBC for what were called "conceptual differences." He moved to WXRK in the coveted morning time slot. The popular New York rock station known as K-Rock would become home not only to Howard Stern but also to Quivers, Norris, Dell'Abate, and the whole Stern radio family for many years to come. Upon starting off in the morning slot, Stern vowed to beat Don Imus in the ratings. Before long he had indeed moved ahead of Imus to the top spot in all of New York radio.

Stern also appreciated the greater freedom K-Rock afforded him. His battle for freedom of speech had given him greater license than ever before, and he had expanded the airwaves with his frank openness and honesty. However, the FCC was not always onboard with Stern's approach to radio. The war for freedom of speech had only just begun.

NOTES

1. Answers.com Web site. "Who2 Biography: Howard Stern, Radio Personality," http://www.answers.com/topic/howard-stern.

2. Peter Castro, "A Stern Upbringing," *People*, November 10, 2003.

3. Newsday Web site. "Howard Stern," 1993, http://www.newsday.com/community/guide/lihistory/ny-hometown_stern,0,2669272.story.

4. Howard Stern, "It Was the Worst of Times, It Was the Worst of Times," in *Private Parts* (New York: Simon & Schuster, 1993), 23–62.

5. Howard Stern, "It Was the Worst of Times, It Was the Worst of Times," in *Private Parts* (New York: Simon & Schuster, 1993), 23–62.

6. Who's Dated Who.com Web site. "Howard Stern, Celebrity Quotes" (originally from IMBD.com) http://www.whosdatedwho.com/celebrity/quotes/howard-stern.htm.

7. Carol F., personal interview with Rich Mintzer, February 2009.

8. Gawker.com Web site. Posting by Jesse, "No Love for Howard in Boston," September 1, 2005, gawker.com/news/howard-stern/no-love-for-howard-in-boston-123452.php.

9. CharlieRose.com Web site. "An Interview with Howard Stern," March 28, 1997, http://www.charlierose.com/view/interview/5637.

10. FamousDJs.com Web site. "Howard Stern biography, 2008," http://www.famousdjs.com/celebs/howard_stern.htm.

11. Brad Dunn, *When They Were 22: 100 Famous People at the Turning Point in Their Lives* (Riverside, NJ: Andrews McMeel Publishing, 2006), 145–46.

12. Chaunce Hayden, "Laughing Her Way to the Top: Robin Quivers Speaks Out!" *Steppin' Out Magazine*, May 1995, 3.

13. Essortment.com Web site. "The Air Florida Crash of Flight 90," http://www.essortment.com/all/airfloridaplan_rjgw.htm.

14. Howard Stern radio show, November 5, 2007.

15. Associated Press, "Don Imus Comment About Pacman Misunderstood," June 23, 2008, available at http://www.foxnews.com Monday 6/28/2008.

Chapter 2

SYNDICATION, THE FCC, TELEVISION, AND POLITICS

Howard Stern was indeed talked about in radio circles, and he had made a name for himself in several markets, but it wasn't until the syndication deal in 1986 that a much larger audience would learn what all the fuss was about. Syndication meant stations in other parts of the country paid the company that owned and created *The Howard Stern Show* to add the show to their lineup. Once in local markets, the stations could then sell advertising to local sponsors. By the fall of 1986, *The Howard Stern Show* was broadcast on WYSP, a rock station in Philadelphia. By late 1988, the show was heard on WJFK-FM in Washington, D.C., a city in which Stern already had many fans from his on-air days in the early 1980s. In time, the show would reach more than a dozen major markets through syndication, including Los Angeles, where some radio critics did not expect Stern to be as successful as he was in the Eastern cities. They were proven wrong, as *The Howard Stern Show* did very well in Los Angeles, the second biggest media market behind New York City.

Besides increasing his audience to a national level, questionable content now had many more program directors looking for hair pieces to cover the rapidly emerging bald spots where they'd torn their hair out. Yes, Howard Stern brought tremendous ratings, and sponsors loved the idea that their commercials would be heard by many more listeners than ever before, but worried program directors and sponsors were never sure when Stern and his cohorts would come up with his next R-rated phone call or questionable on-air game. The shows evoked phone calls of complaints from some listeners, though others thought it was terrific radio—funny, risqué, and unpredictable. Whether they loved him or hated him, Stern's audience was growing, and the switchboard at every station on which he was heard was constantly lit up.

One popular segment that emerged in the late 1980s came from the hiring of John Melendez, who was known on air as Stuttering John. Like Stern, Melendez also hailed from Long Island, where he was often picked on as a youngster because of his stuttering problems. An intern at the Stern show recommended hiring John to conduct interviews. In no time, Stuttering John gained notoriety for asking top celebrities very personal and unusual questions that most interviewers would not dare ask. Some celebrities were offended but most played along. For example, the Dalai Lama laughed when Melendez asked if anyone ever greeted him with "Hello Dolly," as in the classic Broadway musical. Another time he asked former Beatles drummer Ringo Starr what he did with the money his mother gave him for singing lessons. Although it was a backhanded insult, Ringo went with the joke. Stuttering John became a regular on the show for several years, and his popularity eventually led him to work on the *Tonight Show* with Jay Leno.

THE RATINGS KEEP GETTING BETTER

Although content was often on the edge of what was considered in bad taste, the ratings topped the morning market in each city in which the show was heard. Ratings for radio shows are obtained by Arbitron Incorporated, a Maryland-based media research firm that measures network and local market radio audiences in the United States Radio stations use the numbers to demonstrate the size of their audience to potential sponsors who may be interested in advertising on a radio station during a specified time slot or on a specific show. One ratings point can allow a station to charge thousands of dollars more for commercials as they will be heard by thousands of additional listeners.[1]

Some sponsors did not want to place ads during *The Howard Stern Show* because they thought the content would be offensive to potential customers. Many others couldn't wait to be heard by the largest audience in the market, so there was never a shortage of sponsors waiting for time on Stern's program. As a result, Stern was given a longer leash and afforded much more latitude to do what he wanted on air than many other radio personalities. The bottom line was that radio is big business, and Stern's offbeat antics were bringing in big bucks for the stations that dared syndicate his show.

JACKIE "THE JOKEMAN" MARTLING

Adding to the raunchiness of *The Howard Stern Show* was Jackie Martling, who was hired in 1986. Another Long Islander, Martling had gained a local following playing Long Island comedy clubs. His comedy act typically included dirty jokes and grade-school bathroom humor. Martling typically got angry at the audiences for groaning more than laughing at his routine. Nonetheless, he was unrelenting in his desire to make it as a performer and worked constantly at comedy clubs while spending hours recording and hyping his comedy albums of mostly tasteless jokes.

In time, Martling honed his joke-writing ability (still in the bathroom and and tasteless genre) and attracted the attention of Rodney Dangerfield, who used dirtier and raunchier material in his nightclub act than on his television appearances. A giant in the comedy business, Dangerfield bought numerous jokes from Martling. For Martling, however, the big break came when he started writing and even rattling off jokes on air for the very popular Rick Dees Morning Show on KIIS-FM in Los Angeles. Like Stern, Dees was at the top of his market, doing an outrageous morning show on the other side of the country. Stern, however, thought Dees was an amateur and his humor was corny, a charge that was hard to dispute as Dees had released a megahit single called "Disco Duck" in 1976.

Stern has always had a soft spot for tasteless and bodily function jokes, acknowledging that although they may be a bit juvenile, they make him laugh. He knew about Martling, who had built a career based on such jokes.

By the time Martling joined the Stern show as a writer, it was evident that his ability to write tasteless jokes was superior to his ability as a stand-up comic, and he soon became known for inserting jokes onto Stern's show, often writing lines while the show was on air and passing them to Stern. Martling gave the show another source of comedy material. In 2001, he left over a contract dispute.

THE FCC AND CENSORSHIP

During these early years as a syndicated radio host, Stern was carefully watched by the FCC, an independent U.S. government agency (formed by the Communications Act of 1934) that regulates international and interstate communications by radio, television, wire, satellite, cable, and the Internet. The FCC's jurisdiction covers the

50 states, the District of Columbia, and U.S. possessions. The FCC's various bureaus are responsible for processing applications for licenses and other filings, analyzing complaints, conducting investigations, and taking part in hearings.[2]

The FCC oversees the program content to determine whether there is anything improper or indecent. There are certain no-nos, such as cursing on broadcast radio or television. But in addition to certain strict rules and regulations there are judgment calls, where it is up to the FCC to determine whether what was broadcast was considered indecent. Stern and his staffers knew what they clearly could not say on the air, but on numerous incidents they treaded that fine line of what might be considered good taste. Typically, if nobody (meaning listeners or sponsors) complained, the FCC would not make an issue out of what was being aired. However, when complaints started pouring into the FCC offices about *The Howard Stern Show*, they had to take action. In fact, the FCC received more complaints about content of *The Howard Stern Show* than they had received regarding any radio show ever aired. On-air games like You Bet Your Ass, which parodied the old television game show *You Bet Your Life,* and revealing interviews with strippers and porn actresses drew millions of listeners—and drew the attention of FCC officials.

After a December 1988 show in which a guest played the piano with his penis, the FCC levied its first fine at *The Howard Stern Show*. Stern was outraged because this was radio and nobody could see the alleged piano-playing incident. The $6,000 fine was only the beginning. In the ensuing years, the FCC fined Clear Channel Radio, the company that owned Infinity Broadcasting, which was responsible for syndicating the Stern program, upwards of $3 million because of Stern's on-air antics, including such games as Homeless Hollywood Squares or the Lesbian Dating Game. Stern constantly complained about the FCC's censorship on the air, explaining that he was not breaking the rules and was not saying curse words or anything else that was not permitted on the radio. Meanwhile, Stern was attracting a steadily growing audience of listeners.

Stern and his staff took their work very seriously. Although the content might be racy or of questionable taste to some listeners, the idea was to make the audience laugh, to hold their attention, and to keep them coming back to find out what would happen next. Stern, with Dell'Abate, Norris, Quivers, and Jackie Martling, known also as Jackie the Jokeman, worked long hours trying to put together an edgy show without blatantly violating FCC regulations. If Stern loved his work before the syndication deal, he was now married to it.

Before long the sheer volume of ideas and bits the Stern staff came up with, plus Stern's taking calls from listeners and providing his slant on newsworthy issues, meant the show was exceeding its allotted time slot. Some stations had commitments to other programming, but most let the syndicated show run long because it meant keeping more listeners tuned in. Along with doing the radio show itself, which began at 6 A.M. every weekday from the K-Rock studio in New York City, there were post-show meetings, review sessions, and time spent putting together program sessions, easily a weekly commitment of more than 50 hours for Stern and his crew. For Stern, this meant waking up at 4 A.M. each day.

Stern's critics never cared very much about his hard work ethic or his dedication to providing his audience with a good show. As they saw it, Stern did not provide wholesome entertainment and was polluting the airwaves. Stern has often countered such claims by reminding his critics that he does not force anyone to listen to the program and is simply exercising his rights to speak freely.

Stern has always believed his job is to entertain. He is aware that some of what he does may provoke criticism but believes most people know he is joking and it is all meant to be in fun. At times he has been provoked by critics and various special-interest groups that believe he is destroying morality. One of the most outspoken groups, and a long-time thorn in the side of *The Howard Stern Show*, is the American Family Association, a Christian-based group that claims not to promote censorship but instead their own ideas of traditional family values. They have gone after Stern sponsors for years, getting some to stop advertising. Another group, the American Decency Association (ADA), a nonprofit right-wing Christian organization based in Fremont, Michigan, has also constantly targeted Stern and his radio and television shows. Their mission is to "Educate its members and the general public on matters of decency; to initiate, promote, encourage and coordinate activity designed to safeguard and advance public morality consistent with biblical Christianity."[3]

The group monitored Stern's broadcasts for years and spent countless hours on letter-writing campaigns to sponsors. In the late 1990s, the ADA considered Howard Stern's television show to be subversive and wrote: "Our concern remains that a program like this can lead to similar damaging, desensitizing, degrading, addicting programming. That's the desire of people like Stern—to champion sexual openness—without restraint."[4]

One Stern fan responded to the ADA: "If you don't like his show, you spend an awful lot of time listening to it and documenting everything that is said on it. Aren't you worried that you will be corrupted by his viewpoints? Can't you except [sic] that not everyone is like you? Nobody agrees with everything he says on the show. It is just entertainment and nothing more."[5]

In the end, the ADA pulled about 93 percent of the sponsors away from the Howard Stern television show in a two-year period.

Freedom of speech was not a new battle, and, as noted in the preface, Stern was not the first to fight censorship in the media. The media had grown in the years since Lenny Bruce or the Smothers Brothers, so there was a much larger audience than ever before. As a result, the FCC, based on listener complaints, issued more than 120 indecency fines over the past 40 years, all centering on the issue of freedom of speech.

Although the FCC is an independent government agency, there have been times when the chairman has made an effort to appease his political party by cracking down on what is considered indecency. The problem, however, is that the definition of indecency is vague. Stations are careful to comply with the FCC's specific rules and regulations, or they can face fines or license suspensions. However, it is the gray area that comes into consideration when DJs, performers or talk show hosts discuss certain subject areas without clearly violating one of the specific rules. This is where Howard Stern has zigzagged back and forth over the line on numerous occasions.

For the FCC to consider something obscene it must meet certain criteria. For example, does the material in question describe sexual conduct or activities in an offensive manner? Does the material appeal to a prurient interest? Does the material, taken as a whole, lack serious literary, artistic, political, or scientific value? These are among the questions raised and where the debate often begins. What one person may consider artistic, another may consider obscene. The line between suggestive and offensive material has always been open for debate. Many artists have had paintings and other works of art removed from exhibitions or museums over the same debate of art versus indecency. In the case of radio, it depends largely on who is listening and what their personal sense of morality is.

What compounds the problem is that the FCC cannot monitor even a fraction of the broadcast media in the United States, so they rely largely on the complaints from citizens. The positive aspect of this is that individuals can voice their discontent to a government body that will respond. The downside is that if someone simply enjoys complaining or has a personal dislike of a particular program or broadcaster, he or she can make trouble just for the sake of causing trouble.

In an online essay about the FCC, Sir Charles Burden, British writer and performer, mentions Al Westcott, "a self made watchdog who, on his websites, boasts that '[he] is single handedly responsible for more than $2.1 Million in FCC indecency fines against Howard Stern'." Burden posits that "If there was a governing body to control the commission, people like this could be restricted from complaining for the sake of complaining, and truly indecent programs would be targeted. The FCC was designed to, and should only, take complaints from average people. They shouldn't jump on the fine wagon just because someone with a chip on his shoulder and an agenda to advance decided it was time to hit the phones."[6]

As a syndicated radio star with nearly 25 million listeners, Stern is clearly the highest-profile star to do battle with those seeking to shut down his type of entertainment. It was inevitable that someone like Westcott would make a career of trying to stop the Stern radio express.

Stern has certainly not been alone when it comes to raising the ire of the FCC. Other shock jocks, including Chicago's popular Steve Dahl (whom Stern claims he can't stand), born-again right-wing talk show host Mancow Muller, and Bubba the Love Sponge, have also made repeat appearances on the FCC list of indecency fines. In fact, Bubba's $715,000 fine for talking about sex between cartoon characters topped any of Stern's individual fines. If you can outrage the FCC even more than Stern, you must be doing something right, or wrong, depending on your point of view. Stern was actually impressed by Bubba, enough to later bring him on the show and help build the career of the Love Sponge.

FCC fines have also been levied at radio stations for playing songs by Prince, Eminem, and others that contained inappropriate lyrics. And perhaps the most famous FCC fine was in response to the Janet Jackson Super Bowl half time show in 2004. Viacom/CBS television stations were told to fork over $550,000 for the infamous wardrobe malfunction in which one of the singer's breasts was briefly exposed.

Stern, however, topped the list. From 1991 through 2004, the broadcasting company and radio stations hosting *The Howard Stern Show* were fined 13 times for a total of $2,274,750.

The fines, typically reported on the television news and in the newspapers, stirred further debate over what was and was not considered decent, and both sides had good arguments. Those who sided with Stern believed strongly that he was exercising his freedom of speech in good (not so clean) fun, and that although he was indeed offensive, he was poking fun at everyone, including himself. The opposition remained concerned that he was lowering the standards of what was considered appropriate and that his programming was distasteful. The only middle ground was that both sides agreed Stern's programs were inappropriate for young listeners.

THROUGH IT ALL, STERN CONTINUED TO ROLL

"We're still on the air," Stern would say to Quivers, almost in disbelief, after each new round of FCC fines and complaints. Much to the dismay of many of his critics, the FCC often seemed impervious to the outcry to get Howard Stern off the air. Fines were occasionally dropped or hearings were not followed up. Newspaper headlines only seemed to increase his audience and provide Stern with more fuel for the ongoing feud. Many entertainment reporters caught on to the fact that the battles between Stern and the FCC were making the show bigger and drawing more listeners. They were ready and waiting to see what Stern would say the following morning in his response to each attack and fine. While station managers often feared for their jobs, it almost became a more important challenge, not only for Stern but also for those who put him on the air, to support freedom of speech and not let those who sought censorship win these fights. Stern would attack the FCC and call those who ran the commission names on air, much to the delight of his audience. Meanwhile, he was often worried about whether or not the FCC could actually pull the plug on his show. Whatever the outcome, Stern never went down without a fight.

Despite the uproar over the content, Stern had long mastered the art of pacing the show so each segment held his listeners' attention. He would take his time, address an issue, present a guest or a game, and set up everything much in the way a good salesman makes you anxious to see a product demonstration. He knew how to pique the listener's interest with a long buildup to make a segment more exciting. He also had a feel for when a bit was running too long. Throughout all of the turmoil, Stern had mastered the art of presenting compelling radio.

By the 1990s, the show was attracting more celebrities, including movie and television stars whom Stern would put in the hot seat, and Playboy and Penthouse models who talked openly about sexual activities. With celebrities, Stern always took his own approach, such as asking *Friends* star David Schwimmer, "Have you ever seen any of the women on the show naked," referring to Jennifer Aniston, Courtney Cox Arquette, and Lisa Kudrow. Schwimmer, prepared for such

Stern-style questions, laughed and replied that he had almost walked in on Jennifer Aniston's dressing room a little too soon once while she was finishing getting dressed, but that he had not seen anything. Nobody's personal life was off limits. Sometimes the results of such questions took a serious path, such as when Stern interviewed Guns N' Roses guitarist Slash, who talked about coming clean after many years of drug abuse. Stern pried on serious topics as well as those that would evoke laughs.

Stern also offered his opinions about any topic, be it a frivolous news item or the major political stories of the day, and he would look for a means of presenting his own opinion, especially if it was something others dared not say out loud. Such opinions occasionally got him in trouble; for example, regarding the story of the caning of a young American man overseas, Stern said he thought it would be a good form of criminal punishment in the United States.

Not only were his critics, the FCC, and Al Westcott hanging on Stern's every word, but his wife Alison was also paying close attention, especially with an increasing number of sexy women vying to promote their latest video or magazine photo shoot in the studio. Stern was once quoted as saying, "What's the point of being this famous if you can't see naked women?" (People Magazine November 1, 2003, A Stern Upbringing by Peter Castro, http://www.people.com). Those who know Stern understand that it is part of the show, and although he frequently swore his fidelity to his wife on air, there were times when even Alison called in to censor a segment, to say "enough already!" when he was getting a massage from a stripper. Alison trumped decency groups and the FCC when it came to putting the clamps on Stern.

During these early years of syndication the Stern family also grew. Debra Stern was born in 1986 and Ashley Jade Stern in 1993. While Stern talked in great detail about his life with Alison on the air, his daughters were rarely discussed. He took his role as a parent very seriously and was often described by Alison as a very caring father.

For Stern, the biggest struggle was not with the FCC, but over his own personal schedule. Sleeping from 8 P.M. to 4 A.M. and working long hours left him little family time. To maximize family hours, and because it was not his scene, he did not hang out at celebrity clubs and parties, but opted to go from one of the highest profile media celebrities by day to a very low-profile family man in the New York City suburbs by night. This afforded him the opportunity to spend some quality time with Alison and his girls.

TAKING IT TO TELEVISION

If the FCC had its hands full with Howard Stern on the radio, they knew their job would be as bad, or worse, once Stern hit television. But television was the next logical step for Stern. The problem, however, was the tight schedule. Stern already devoted more than 50 hours a week to his radio show, so creating and producing a television show of the quality he wanted seemed an impossible task. In 1990, his first television effort tried to pull together the radio format plus sketches and versions of some of the on-air games and contests. Although the syndicated program captured a few of the comedic elements of the radio show, it was choppy and looked thrown together.

To make matters worse, the show was the immediate target of the anti-Stern brigade, and they contacted the FCC before, during and after each sketch, joke, or questionable phrase complaining that Stern was presenting a deviant message to the American public. The FCC was slow in responding, but advertisers were scared off by threats of boycotts of their products led by ADA members and other groups.

Although Stern's loyal fans did enjoy the program and it got good ratings for a short time in New York City, it did not last very long (it premiered in New York: July 14, 1990, production ended in July 1992). Ultimately, the cast and crew were stretched too thin to make it work and to fight the ongoing battles. The radio show remained the number one priority for Howard Stern and all those involved.

A few short years later (May 1994) however, the E! Network, entertainment TV, picked up on what Stern does best: his radio show. The network began broadcasting edited 30-minute versions of the daily radio programs directly from the Stern studios at K-Rock in New York City. This worked very well, because the time and effort put into the television show were minimal. Essentially, the radio show continued as it was with the addition of some cameras and lighting. The rest was up to the editors at E! to pull a program together, which generally consisted of the funniest segment of each day's activities. The show was an instant rating grabber. Because this show was heavily edited and was aired on free cable television, there was less of an outcry from Stern's critics.

In 1993, Stern had presented a two-hour pay-per-view television special, *Howard Stern's New Year's Rotten Eve*, an outrageous parody of beauty contests, which drew a huge audience. Stern and his crew had more creative freedom than in previous television attempts because there were no sponsors and the program was not on network television.

They stretched the limits of good taste and good fun further than ever before and produced a program that was tasteless, captivating, and, at times, very funny. The program opened with Howard Stern sitting on the toilet and included:

- Parodies of Michael Jackson and Jerry Seinfeld
- Celebrity judges ranging from actors Sherman Hemsley (*The Jeffersons*) and Mark Hamill (*Star Wars*) to former Ku Klux Klan member Daniel Carver
- A woman reciting erotic poetry
- A woman who poured ice cream all over her body
- A woman who put living maggots on her body

In all, 40 women and one man competed to be crowned Miss Howard Stern, and the top 20 performed on the program. The winner was Elaine Marks, a model who had appeared in *Playboy* magazine a couple of years earlier. Despite being blasted for tastelessness by numerous TV critics, the *New Year's Rotten Eve* event brought in some $40 million in revenue.

Although Stern dabbled in other television projects, and his fans expected annual New Year's Eve pageants, they were not forthcoming. Stern knew that the level of production quality would suffer with too much time divided between other projects, and he was not one to do mediocre work or work with people he did not know or trust.

GOING POLITICAL

In 1994, Stern decided to become involved in politics by running for governor of New York State. This was before the election of several other celebrity governors, including Jesse Ventura, the pro wrestler who became governor of Minnesota in 1999, and Arnold Schwarzenegger, the actor elected governor of California in 2003.

At the time, many people considered Stern's sudden move into the political arena to be nothing more than a publicity stunt or another way of generating more attention. What they did not anticipate was that there was actually a message behind the madness and that Stern actually had some real issues that he wanted to address.

First, Stern was rallying for the death penalty to be reinstated in New York State, which Republicans feared could draw votes away from their candidate if Stern did get on the ballot. Stern also favored fixing New York's potholes at night so that the work did not interfere with daytime traffic and wanted to stagger tolls so that collecting them at the bridges in and out of the city did not incur such massive traffic delays. Sure he made the usual tasteless jokes, such as saying that they could "use the ashes from the executed criminals to fill the potholes," but he was indeed serious about his campaign.

Although many dismissed Stern's campaign as a lark, the Libertarian Party, a small conservative party that had never generated any significant influence, took Stern's campaign seriously enough to help him get on the ballot. Stern had been in contact with the Libertarians for several years before throwing his hat into the governor's race. To get on the ballot, he needed roughly 15,000 valid signatures, which would be very easily attained with Stern's loyal following.[7]

Stern's critics and some political analysts were deeply concerned. Others, however, saw his campaign as a way of getting his messages heard. One stumbling block was the FCC rule mandating that candidates must receive equal time on the media. Because Stern was contracted for numerous hours on the radio and television, his opponents would need to be afforded equal time or Stern's air time would need to be limited.

All of the furor generated what Stern loved most—media attention. Stories appeared in the *New York Times* and other leading papers in the United States and around the world. Kevin Jackson, a writer for Britain's *The Independent*, wrote: "Aspiring Governor Howard Stern— who now rates a more than respectable 20 per cent in unofficial opinion polls—is not the kind of politician who would normally go down well in Middle America. For one thing, there's his appearance, closer to a pensioned-off bassist for Aerosmith or Bon Jovi than a dark-suited pillar of the Right." He added, "For another, there's his mouth, and the unsavory things that come tumbling out of it . . . dwelling on bodily functions, bragging about his talents, denigrating the latest celebrity to have won his disfavor, making incendiary cracks about racial issues and generally offending against good taste."[8]

For someone so many loved to hate, Stern had reached a point in his career where the media seemed to be waiting on his every move— something that continues to this day.

Despite his serious political intentions, Stern promised that should he win, he would resign the moment he achieved his three-part platform. "It doesn't matter if you find me offensive," he said the morning he announced his candidacy. "I'll get out of office before I can really screw anything up" ("Gov. Howard Stern? Some Fail to See Humor" by Todd S. Purdum, April 3, 1994, *New York Times*; available at http://www.nytimes.com/1994/04/03/us/gov-howard-stern-some-fail-to-see-humor.html?pagewanted=all).

In the end, however, Stern withdrew from the race for governor because, by law, candidates need to disclose how much money they earn, and he did not want to make his earnings public. Stern's brief venture into politics once again gave him the opportunity to speak out and exercise his right to voice his ideas and concerns, some of which were picked up by other politicians. In 1995, New York governor George Pataki signed into law the Howard Stern Bill, which restricted construction to nighttime on state roads on Long Island and in New York City.

ONLY SO MANY HOURS IN THE DAY

The syndication of his show to numerous national markets moved Stern from a local DJ with a local following to a national household name synonymous with radio. His ongoing battles with the FCC and his ability to straddle the fine line between good and bad taste was indeed making him a champion of freedom of speech. Of course, Stern always proclaimed that he was not doing what he did to promote freedom of speech; he simply wanted to put on the best show possible, and anyone who knew him agreed that Stern's goal was simply to do great radio.

The syndication of his radio show and the nightly E! broadcasts enhanced the already growing media circus that surrounded the world of Howard Stern. Reporters were always on the prowl to find out what he was up to and what he would dare do next. His cohorts, especially his producer Gary Dell'Abate, were entrusted with keeping a lid on the Stern show plans, and Stern remained tight-lipped about his personal life.

Hounded for interviews and receiving numerous offers to appear at celebrity gatherings, Stern continued to steer clear of anything that would affect his time spent working on the radio show. First and foremost, Stern remained obsessed with staying at the top of his field, so he worked tirelessly to entertain his legions of listeners. The commitment to his career was unwavering, although it would eventually take its toll on his marriage. Nonetheless, he acknowledged many times over the years that he was indeed obsessive compulsive and as a result a workaholic.

Somewhere in the midst of it all, Howard Stern found time to write his first book, an autobiographical account, with rants, photos, and other tidbits tossed in, called *Private Parts*. The book, the subsequent reactions, and the film of the same name will be the focus of the next chapter.

NOTES

1. For an explanation of ratings points, go to the Arbitron Web site, http://www.arbitronratings.com.

2. An explanation of the Federal Communications Commission is found on their Web site, http://www.fcc.gov.

3. This quote is from the American Decency Association Web site, Mission Statement, http://www.americandecency.org.

4. American Decency Association Web site, excerpt from the Section on Howard Stern, http://www.americandecency.org.

5. American Decency Association Web site, excerpt from the Blog on Howard Stern http://www.americandecency.org.

6. This quote is from Sir Charles Burden, "Federal Censorship Corporation," http://rationalwiki.com/wiki/Essay:FCC.

7. Todd S. Purdom, "Gov. Howard Stern? Some Fail to See Humor," *New York Times*, April 3, 1994, http://www.nytimes.com/1994/04/03/us/gov-howard-stern-some-fail-to-see-humor.html.

8. Quoted material from Kevin Jackson, "The Candidate Has Landed," *The Independent*, Life & Style Section, May 14, 1994.

Chapter 3

BRANCHING OUT:
BEST-SELLING BOOKS, A HIT
FILM (PLUS A VERY SCARY FAN)

In 1993, Howard Stern's autobiography, *Private Parts*, was released by Simon and Schuster. The book spent five weeks on top of the *New York Times* best seller list and became the fastest seller in the long and esteemed history of Simon and Schuster.

Private Parts, which allowed Stern to describe his childhood in his own words—such as, "My father's favorite sport was yelling"[1]—is Stern's personal take on his own experiences, including his awkward teenage years and meeting Alison. He describes his radio career and his ongoing battles with authorities in his attempt to do his own show his own way.

The book also presents Stern's opinions on everything from the French and gays to various celebrities who irritate him, such as Oprah Winfrey and Arsenio Hall. Interspersed are lesbian stories, for which Stern has always had a great passion, and some interesting photos. Stern's goal was to capture his story, his personality, and his penchant for comedy and sexy women all in one volume.

Naturally, the book became the center of great debate and led to another battle of art versus censorship. No matter how many copies the book sold, the anti-Stern rabble-rousers had their usual complaints: too vulgar, full of juvenile humor, tasteless, and so on.

CRITICS ARE DIVIDED

In one review, from the *Washington Monthly*, Scott Shuger said of Simon & Schuster's editing of the book: "There's utterly no evidence of shaping or guidance . . . The result is that *Private Parts* isn't about anything. Or to be more accurate, it's all about Howard Stern, and he isn't about anything."[2]

The book did garner some positive reviews. In *Entertainment Weekly*, Owen Gleiberman called Stern "the most brilliant—and misunderstood—comic artist in America." For Gleiberman, Stern is "the Lenny Bruce of the information age," and "probably the only professional entertainer in the country who answers to no one but himself." "What his fans cherish is his blessedly untamed hilarity, the rollicking freedom of his voice," Gleiberman writes. "This blasphemously funny autobiography-scrapbook is, in essence, Stern's radio show jammed between two covers."[3]

Clearly, Gleiberman had an understanding of what Howard Stern was all about before the book, but by the time the book came out in 1993, most people's minds were made up. You either liked Howard Stern or you didn't, and the book was not about to change very many opinions.

The book set off its own censorship concerns. Caldor's, a discount store selling mostly various household goods, posted its own censored version of the *New York Times* best seller list by removing Stern's book from the number one spot and moving numbers 2 through 11 up a notch.[4]

Stern, along with Simon and Schuster, were particularly clever about marketing and selling the book. For example, when the book was released in paperback, roughly 60 pages were added with new and updated information, primarily reactions to the original release. The paperback also had two versions of the cover, each featuring half of Stern's face. This meant that truly devoted Stern fans had to buy two copies to get the whole photo, and some hardcore Stern fans did just that.

The book also stirred up some controversy in Westlaco, Texas, a small city of less than 30,000 people, where librarian Pam Antonelli was fired for putting the book in the library. Antonelli later appeared on the television talk show *Donahue* with Howard Stern and a lawyer representing Westlaco. She went on to sue the city and ended up settling out of court.[5]

Book banning is one of the most frequent challenges of the First Amendment. For decades, books have been pulled from library shelves and classrooms because someone complains that a book is unsuitable for some reason and has challenged the school or library. These are books that, to some individuals or groups, are considered too controversial, unorthodox, or inappropriate for young readers. Challenging the notion of banning books, the American Library Association (ALA), the American Booksellers Association (ABA), and various other groups have even begun sponsoring banned book weeks to back up such freedom of expression. According to the ALA, books "usually are challenged with the best intentions—to protect others, frequently children, from difficult ideas and information." [6]

The three major reasons for challenging books are, in descending order, sexual explicitness, offensive language, and "unsuited to a particular age group." Other reasons include occult themes, violence, promotion of homosexuality, promotion of a religious viewpoint, nudity, racism, presentation of sex education, and books considered "anti-family." The challenges come from both the right and left ends of the political spectrum. According to the ALA, most challenges are made by parents, and most are unsuccessful.

Ironically, many of the books that were once banned are now on school reading lists. Greater acceptance in society (in some parts of the country) and greater cultural awareness, especially regarding issues of race, and acceptance of various lifestyles, are now allowing such once banned books to be widely accepted in most schools and libraries. Among the more famous banned books now found on classroom reading lists are *The Catcher in the Rye* and *To Kill A Mockingbird*. From Mark Twain, to Maya Angelou, to J.K. Rowling, Howard Stern found himself in esteemed company with his first ever book when he checked in at number 87 on the American Library Association's Office for Intellectual Freedom List of the 100 Most Frequently Challenged Books of 1990–2001.[6]

The overall success of the book did not surprise those who knew the sheer size of the Stern fan base throughout the country, in particular the markets carrying the daily radio programs. In New York City, a single book signing drew some 50,000 people to a midtown book store, blocking traffic and causing some degree of chaos. Perhaps what surprised some of Stern's critics was that many of the book buyers were well-educated, successful businessmen and women. It was typically assumed that Stern fans were sophomoric, nonreading underachievers, slackers, freaks, weirdos, and degenerates. Although this group makes up some of the audience, Howard Stern fans come from all walks of life.

ONE MORE TIME

The success of *Private Parts* prompted Stern to do a follow-up of sorts two years later: the book *Miss America*. Once again, there was some censorship fighting from the onset. The book was originally titled *Getting Away With Murder*, and the cover depicted Stern with O.J. Simpson at Donald Trump's wedding. The publishers backed off from the possible uproar such a cover might have caused and went instead with a photo of Howard Stern dressed in drag. The second book became the fastest-selling book in publishing history when it was released in 1995. *Miss America* had a greater focus on Stern's radio career than the first book. Though it was not as big a seller as *Private Parts*, the book still sold millions of copies to fans, admirers, and those still curious about the ever-changing world of Howard Stern.

Miss America takes a tough look at a number of subjects, from Stern's hair to Stuttering John to life in the radio business. It was an opportunity to let loose on celebrities Stern couldn't stand, or understand. For example, he describes his initial meeting with Michael Jackson, where he tore into the controversial former pop star for being weird. Stern also delves into his own radio family, which by the mid-1990s had grown in size and significance to the program. Perhaps it was because the previous book was his first venture into publishing or because Stern, by this time, had revealed so much about himself on the radio, but *Miss America* did not generate the same amount of press—positive or negative—as the previous book.

LIGHTS, CAMERA, ACTION

Stern's tremendous popularity made him a potential choice for many movie roles, but the scripts that came his way over the years, many from small independent film companies, did not interest him. Stern did not want to jump into a film career by making a bad movie, knowing that whatever he did would generate a lot of attention and that his acting skills were limited at best. At one point Stern was signed to a deal with New Line Cinema to make a movie out of his Fartman character, which he had introduced to the world in an infamous appearance at the *1992 MTV Music Video Awards*. Complete in his Fartman costume, with bare buttocks blurred for the television broadcast, Stern shocked the crowd at the start of the awards show by descending on a rope to the stage below while portraying American's latest and most crass superhero. In time, the project was canceled over what was said to be a rights issue to the Fartman character.

Ultimately, Stern found the role of a lifetime playing himself in the film version of *Private Parts*. Although it might seem very easy to simply play yourself on camera, as Stern would learn, it was far more difficult than he imagined. Because movies are made with a well-developed storyline, in this case taken from his autobiography, his freedom to be himself would be limited by the need to move the storyline forward in roughly 90 minutes, less than a single Stern radio broadcast. Making a film also meant following a script and shooting short scenes, often out of order. Stern was used to a stream of consciousness format, interrupted only for commercials, in which he was able to keep on talking, switching subjects, and remaining in complete control of what was going on in his own comfortable environment. Being part of a movie, with a huge crew on hand and significantly more equipment all around him, was going to be a very different experience.

Turning an offbeat autobiography, with some questionable content, into a major motion picture with a star who had never acted on the big screen before would be a major challenge. Fortunately, Ivan Reitman, a Stern fan, stepped up to produce the film. Reitman was already an accomplished filmmaker with a long line of successes. The Czechoslovakian-born producer/director had been the creative force behind a number of comedy hits, including the classic frat house epic *Animal House* and the Bill Murray films *Meatballs*, *Stripes,* and *Ghostbusters.* He also brought out a softer, gentler side of tough guy Arnold Schwarzenegger in the films *Twins* and *Kindergarten Cop.* Reitman had worked with another major star with little acting experience—basketball player Michael Jordan in *Space Jam.*[7] With Reitman in charge, what Stern lacked in experience was made up for by having a consummate professional at the helm.

Getting the right script was next on the agenda. Stern rejected many versions before finally working with accomplished screenwriter Len Blum to pull the right material from the book for the feature film. The goal was to include Stern's story while also putting some of the funny parts of the book on the screen.

The last piece to the puzzle was finding a director who understood Howard Stern's humor and had the patience to work with an actor who was admittedly out of place in front of a film crew. Betty Thomas was brought in for the job. After a career as an actress in movies such as *Tunnel Vision* and *Used Cars* and on the hit television drama *Hill Street Blues* in the early 1980s, Thomas had turned to directing. She had directed a hit television series on HBO, *Dream On,* and films such as *The Brady Bunch Movie* before accepting the role of director on *Private Parts,* which was scheduled for shooting in 1996.[8]

The making of *Private Parts* brought out Stern's insecurities as he was away from his comfort zone behind the microphone. On more than

one occasion he was ready to quit the film and call off the whole project. He routinely asked Betty Thomas if she thought he was an actor,
and she would provide encouragement. Having worked long and hard
to get to the number one position in radio, and having changed the
face of the medium, Stern did not want to go before the cameras and
embarrass himself. So, Thomas worked closely with Stern on how to
stay in the character and how to interact with his costars, such as
Robin Quivers and Fred Norris, who were playing themselves; Mary
McCormack, who played his wife, Alison; and Paul Giamatti.

A SUPPORTING HAND

Michael Gwynne, a long-time television and film actor with many
small roles in big films, had perhaps a bigger impact on the film than
his small role might have indicated. He talked about his experience on
the set and what it was like working with Stern.

Gwynne had met Betty Thomas in 1982 on the set of *Hill Street
Blues*, and they had remained friends. When Thomas began putting the
pieces together for *Private Parts*, she recalled that Gwynne had been a
radio DJ for many years before launching his acting career and asked
him to take a look at the script. As Gwynne recalls, "She also
explained that Stern was terrified. He had never been an actor, and she
really did not want him crashing on the set or falling apart. She knew I
had done radio and thought that perhaps having me around as a safety
device to talk radio might be helpful to Stern to keep him in his comfort zone."

Gwynne was offered the role of a generic, experienced DJ—the Duke
of Rock—at the radio station in Detroit where Stern started out. As a
veteran DJ who had moved around a lot, Gwynne related to the character, so he took the role and headed to Silver Cup Studios in Long
Island City in Queens, New York.

"We started in a big ballroom where the entire cast sat around a
huge horseshoe table and read through the script. Stern was very
uncomfortable, but like a good reader, which he always was, like radio
people are, he read the lines and he got through it. On about page 40,
I chimed in as the Duke of Rock in my best radio DJ voice and from
that point forward I became known to the cast, the crew and Stern, as
'the Duke,'" explains Gwynne.

The first day of shooting, "I remember getting to the studio in a
limo, and when I arrived it was chaotic, which is normal for a film
shoot, with everyone running around doing something. Stern was

wearing a stupid wig which gave him the younger look for the scene. He was walking around the control room mock-up they had built for us. He looked nervous and did not look particularly happy, but we got into a conversation about the soundboard. I told him it reminded me of a 1959 or 1962 board. Once we started talking about radio, he seemed to relax," recalls Gwynne.

Gwynne was impressed that Stern never complained. Gwynne had seen his share of big egos in action—making demands and insisting things be done a certain way—but Stern was smart enough to know that he didn't know everything in this situation. "He put himself in a position to let things happen rather than making the mistake a lot of big stars make by trying to be in control all of the time," added Gwynne. It was, perhaps, Stern's insecurity that allowed Thomas to work with him successfully and help him ease his way into the role and the scenes.

For the scene between Stern and Gwynne, Thomas let them try several approaches. In the short scene, the Duke of Rock is on the air finishing up his overnight shift when Stern comes in with a box of tricks, or sound effects, which were used often by DJs of the era. The Duke says, "Hey, it's the new guy coming up next. Look at this guy. He looks like Big Bird." The Duke then signs off with an old radio phrase, "If you can't be good, be bad," and turns the microphone over to Stern. Gwynne ad-libbed the line "Whatever you do, don't hurt yourself" before departing. "[Stern] was delighted that we were playing guys from the '70s and he got it. . . . he wasn't the big 'star' who wanted to do it again and again. He recalled what it was like in his early days of radio and got the scene immediately," recalls Gwynne. Less than a minute long, the scene was shot several times over four days. Because Stern had to be up early for his radio show, he could not stay later than around 4 P.M., so shooting days were cut short.

During the long stretches of downtime, Gwynne recalls that he and Stern talked about the radio business and swapped stories of the early days on the road in small town after small town. Although Gwynne's on-screen role was brief, he had achieved what Betty Thomas wanted: being another radio guy for Stern to talk with and around whom he could relax and get away from the worries of acting.

"Howard was intuitively a good actor. What he got, and a lot of people don't get, is the separation of themselves from the idea of the characters. He knew it was about reproducing himself as a guy on the radio who was starting out and was terrible. At that time you had to have the radio voice and be 'hip,' and Howard wasn't. So instead he broke the taboos of language, of form and of structure. He broke all the rules, like Salvador Dali the artist. He got fired a lot, but each time he got fired, the station managers would realize the ratings had gotten better [with Stern]. And every time he got fired and moved somewhere else he got more popular. Eventually, they were paying him millions of dollars just to be who he is," explains Gwynne of Stern. [9]

When the film opened, it had a gala premiere at the famed Ziegfeld Theater on Manhattan's West Side. This was a red carpet event featuring the cast and crew of the movie plus the stars of the radio show, several of whom, such as Robin Quivers and Fred Norris, played themselves on screen. It was a hot ticket, and thousands of fans lined the streets around the theater in support of their hero—and waited for the reviews.

Private Parts not only pleased the Stern fans but also played very well to a mainstream audience, many of whom never expected to like the film. Stern's vulnerability as a shy, awkward, geeky teenager made him likable, and his on-screen romance with Mary McCormack as Alison was authentic and touching. It revealed how Alison understood Stern and was supportive while he genuinely needed her love and approval. The rough spots in their relationship and his need to tell the public everything about their personal life put their relationship to the test, but it all worked in the end. Sure, the movie contained raunchy moments, as one would expect from Stern, but it was hard for audiences not to root for him as the movie depicted how the geeky teenager built a career as a major radio star.

Stern likened the film to a Rocky-like story of an unlikely hero making it big, and it played as such. The movie was well-received by critics, even those who were ready to hate it. In fact, some critics seemed disappointed that Reitman, Thomas, and Stern had made such a likable film. The movie did very well at the box office, although it did not achieve the blockbuster success of the book.

Peter Travers, long-time movie reviewer for *Rolling Stone* magazine (http://www.movlic.com/publicity/Synopsis/0015350.html), wrote "*Private Parts* is a comic firecracker with a surprising human touch" while the *LA Times* review (http://www.metacritic.com/video/titles/privateparts) was also quite positive: "*Private Parts* is supremely crafty, smartly written, and—given the number of 'himselfs' and 'herselfs' on the cast list—is surprisingly well-acted." Even the *New York Times*, often highly critical of such comedies, had good things to say: "Thanks to sharp editing and surprisingly strong comic timing, the film puts less emphasis on the Stern raunchiness than on how his wilder routines make listeners drive off the road." Of those who didn't like the film, the *Washington Post*'s Desson Thomson wrote (www.washingtonpost. com), "Unfortunately, the movie is likely to earn more money than praise. If it showcases [Stern] in all his glory, it also shows what little glory there is to celebrate."

Robert Firsching, from the online All Movie Guide (from http:// www.answers.com/topic/private-parts-film-1), considered the film to be a romantic comedy. "Although this biographical comedy about famed shock jock Howard Stern has all the raunch his fans would expect, it is also a remarkably moving love story."

Firsching referred to the relationship between Howard and Alison, which made the movie much more touching than Stern's raunchier fans might have liked but drew a larger audience of nonfans who were pleasantly surprised.

For someone like Stern, there is usually a big gap between his fans and his harshest critics. Yet somehow a film from a book that had drawn a wide range of responses from "great" to "disgusting" managed to find a middle ground thanks to some excellent (and seasoned) professionals such as Ivan Reitman and Betty Thomas. For his role in *Private Parts*, Stern won a Blockbuster Entertainment Award—an award based on fan votes—for Favorite Male Newcomer in 1997.

Stern has never ventured onto the big screen again, though plenty of film offers followed, mostly for cameo appearances in other people's films. Such offers have, thus far, not interested him. The combination of hard work to put on the radio show, not to mention all of the other activities that would later take precedence in his life, have kept his screen acting career at a minimum, although Stern has joked that he is "the world's laziest movie star."

THE FRIGHTENING COST OF FAME

One of the downsides to being controversial and in the public eye is the risk of attracting the wrong kind of attention. For example, in recent years many celebrities have had to deal with the problem of stalkers, some of whom may be dangerous. John Hinckley, for example, became famous for stalking actress Jodie Foster. In an effort to gain her attention, he tried to assassinate President Ronald Reagan in 1981. David Letterman, host of *Late Night* on CBS television, had a stalker who was found sleeping on his private tennis courts and arrested, while actress Catherine Zeta-Jones received death threats from a woman who threatened to slice her up.[10] Britney Spears, Avril Lavigne, Tom

Cruise, and other celebrities have also had stalkers tracked down by the police. Depending on how far the stalker goes and how menacing he or she is, the result can range from a restraining order to an arrest and conviction.

For Howard Stern one stalker went too far. Michael Lance Carvin sent numerous hate-filled letters to Stern, threatening to kill not only the radio star but also Stern's wife. Carvin started sending a series of letters and postcards to Stern at the K-Rock studios, calling Stern a "dead man walking" and adding, "I will absolutely, without a doubt, kill you. And this is 100% guaranteed."[11]

Carvin was not unknown to authorities. In 1975, he had been arrested for pulling a toy gun on Ronald Reagan after he announced his first presidential campaign. Carvin was later arrested and spent six years in jail for threatening to kill former President Gerald Ford and Vice President Nelson Rockefeller.

The threats to Stern began in January 1997 and continued for several months. Although he did not address the issue on the air, Stern grew more concerned over these threats than he was about some of his typical hate mail. According to reports from the trial, Stern even received a letter containing a fuse and a flammable material with the note, "You can get your head blown off opening the mail." Soon after, in late April, Carvin switched his attention to Alison, threatening to slit her throat. Carvin was finally arrested on April 29, 1997, and was sentenced to two and a half years in prison in January 1998.[11]

EXECUTIVE PRODUCER HOWARD STERN

Though Stern's television show on E! continued to draw excellent ratings, giving viewers an edited version of what went on each day in the studio, and featured the more visual aspects of the program, including scantily clad female guests playing some odd games, Stern took on another television project. In 1999, he began work on a sitcom for the FX network, a cable channel with a limited audience and few original programs.

Serving in a behind-the-scenes role, Stern created a series called *Son of a Beach*. A parody of *Baywatch*, a popular hit series of that time, the Stern-produced sitcom featured the same premise of lifeguards on the beach, only the lead male character, unlike *Baywatch* star David Hasselhoff, was overweight and out of shape. Nearly everything on the show was a pun, cliché, or groaner of a joke. Described by some TV critics as cheesy and by some viewers as "so bad it was good," the series ran for roughly 45 episodes before being canceled. It did have its share of out-of-work guest stars, ranging from Mark Hamill to Erik Estrada, Gary Coleman, Joey Buttafuoco (famous for his well-publicized affair with teenager Amy Fisher, who tried to kill his wife), and Patty Hearst, whose kidnapping was one of the most riveting news stories of 1974.

However, even with offbeat celebrities; a costar, Jaime Bergman, who was featured twice in Playboy magazine; and plenty of double entendre jokes the series was canceled. Without Stern on camera, clearly something was missing.

Meanwhile, as Stern took to behind-the-scenes television production in the late 1990s, Robin Quivers stepped into a few television guest star roles. In 1993, she appeared on *The Fresh Prince of Bel Air*, playing alongside series star Will Smith. In 1996, fresh off her own autobiographical best-selling book, she took on a bigger role, costarring in a made-for-television movie, *Deadly Web*. However, like Stern, she has little energy left for acting roles after putting in long hours on the radio and at staff meetings.

KING OF ALL MEDIA

As the 1990s drew to a close, Stern had indeed made good on his self-proclaimed title, King of All Media. He had branched out from radio with two best-selling books, a successful film debut, and two television programs. Unlike so many entertainers, Stern somehow managed to stay on top, while many of his radio contemporaries came and went, enjoying their 15 minutes of fame.

FCC fines, and there would be more to come in the upcoming decade, were part of what kept Stern on top. Each time another fine was announced, fans and nonfans tuned in to hear his response. There's an old saying, "there's no such thing as bad publicity," and for Stern it was so true. Stern had a forum from which to speak out, vent his frustrations, and respond to critics—a nationally syndicated radio show and a television show.

Always one to enjoy doing self-promotion, Stern visited his friend David Letterman on his late night talk show from time to time. Letterman understood what Stern was all about, and his own dry sense of humor was a perfect foil for Stern. They were almost like two kids trying not to get into trouble as the audience (and censors) watched carefully to see that they behaved themselves. The idea that Stern could stretch the limits at any given moment always made him an alluring guest. Even when Stern carefully talked around topics that were questionable for television, the audience knew exactly where he was headed, and Letterman had no intention of stopping him.

The potential for high ratings or increased sales also meant there was always a long list of interviewers who wanted to book some time with Stern. Although he did not do many interviews, he occasionally sat down and responded to questions about anything interviewers chose to ask. The only subject Stern kept off limits was his income and accumulated wealth—he tried to keep those areas out of the conversation in an effort not to separate himself too much from his legion of fans. Of course, newspaper journalists would get the inside scoop on Stern's latest contracts, and rough figures (now in the millions) would surface in print. Nonetheless, Stern did not want to discuss money.

During most interviews Stern remained humble, even somewhat surprised at his own success. He was well aware of his shortcomings when he entered the radio field but was also very proud of his accomplishments. Sporting both bravado and a vulnerable side, Stern was an interesting subject for an interview. Some of his answers (from his bio on the International Movie Database, at http://www.us.imdb.com/name/nm0001769/bio) were extreme, such as when he quipped that there should be no one on radio except for him, or when asked about his favorite kind of music, he'd say, "I like music that makes me want to kill myself," referring to his passion for heavy metal. Some of his answers were heartfelt, such as those about his relationship with Alison and his desire to be a good parent and spend more time with his daughters. His responses were genuine, not staged or scripted, which was also the case with most of his banter on the radio.

By 2000, Stern and his radio family knew how to play off of each other for better and for worse. Sometimes shows would cover personal stories of Dell'Abate, Quivers, Norris, or others involved with the show. They teased each other, fought with each other, and sometimes even took care of each other. Unlike most celebrity casts, the core group was together day in and day out for years. In fact, they are still together. One's life was an open book once one was part of the Stern radio family. It was reality radio long before reality television ever emerged. Who would have ever thought that telling the truth would be more interesting than anything else on radio?

As the 1990s drew to a close, what the Stern radio family did not know was that perhaps the most dysfunctional member of the gang would join them only a short time later, someone whose life experiences rivaled anything the regulars could imagine, someone whom they would eventually reprimand, fight with, coddle, take care of and love, while laughing at his tremendous sense of humor. Yes, Artie Lange would join *The Howard Stern Show* in 2001, as discussed in the next chapter, along with the windfall deal that made Howard Stern the highest-paid radio personality in the world.

NOTES

1. Howard Stern, *Private Parts* (New York: Simon & Schuster, 1993), 41.

2. Scott Shuger, "Private Parts–Book Review," *Washington Monthly*, December 1993, http://findarticles.com/p/articles/mi_m1316/is_n12_v25/ai_14737965.

3. Owen Gleiberman, "Exposing Himself," *Entertainment Weekly*, October 22, 1993, http://www.ew.com/ew/article/0,308499,00.html.

4. James Barron, "Stores Shy Away From Book Written by Radio Personality," *The New York Times*, November 12, 1993.

5. The Complete Howard Stern Links! Web site, "Howard Stern Books," http://www.animaux.net/stern/books.html. The Web site http://www.highbeam.com, Highbeam research, has the story from the *Albany Times Union*, October 1, 2004, "Gee Thanks Howard Stern," author n/a.

6. InfoPlease.com, Brunner Borgna. "Books under Fire," http://www.infoplease.com/spot/bannedbookslist.html.

7. Internet Movie Database, "Ivan Reitman," http://www.imdb.com/name/nm0718645/bio.

8. Internet Movie Database, "Betty Thomas," http://www.imdb.com/name/nm0858525/bio.

9. Michael C. Gwynne, Personal interview with the author, May 2009.

10. James Duffy, "Celebrity Stalkers," *Boston Globe*, http://www.bostonglobe.com.

11. Greg B. Smith, "Vow to Kill Stern: Letters Sent to DeeJay & Wife," *New York Daily News*, May 26, 1998, http://www.nydailynews.com/archives/news/1998/05/26/1998-05-26_vow_to_kill_stern_feds__lett.html.

Radio shock jock Howard Stern displays his book Private Parts *at a book-signing appearance in Midtown Manhattan on Oct. 14, 1993. Stern's appearance attracted thousands of fans who jammed Fifth Avenue outside the Barnes and Noble bookstore where he appeared. (AP Photo)*

Helen Trimble, of the Brooklyn borough of New York, embraces a mock-heroic Howard Stern during a news conference in New York on Dec. 7, 1994. Trimble got out of her car on the George Washington Bridge to talk to a distraught man who called Stern's radio show on a cellular phone and threatened to leap from the bridge. (AP Photo/Kathy Willens)

Comedian Chris Rock, left, radio personality Howard Stern and actress Beth
Ostrosky, right, watch the New York Knicks play the Indiana Pacers at Madison
Square Garden in New York on Dec. 8, 2001. (AP Photo/Jeff Zelevansky)

In this photo released by the Hard Rock Cafe, Howard Stern raises his fist in triumph when arriving at the Hard Rock Cafe on Dec. 16, 2005, in New York's Times Square, to celebrate the launch of his career at Sirius Satellite Radio. (AP Photo/Hard Rock Cafe, Diane Bondareff)

Radio shock jock Howard Stern greets the audience at the beginning of the Howard Stern 2006 Film Festival at Hudson Theatre near Times Square in New York on April 27, 2006. (AP Photo/Hiroko Masuike)

Radio show host Howard Stern and girlfriend model Beth Ostrosky attend a Cinema Society-hosted screening of Things We Lost in the Fire *at the Tribeca Grand Hotel in New York on Oct. 6, 2007. (AP Photo/Evan Agostini)*

Howard Stern leaves a taping of "The Late Show with David Letterman" in New York on June 8, 2009. (AP Photo/ Charles Sykes)

Chapter 4

FROM SYNDICATION TO SIRIUS SATELLITE RADIO TO A FILM FESTIVAL: WITH ARTIE BUT WITHOUT ALISON

By 2000, *The Howard Stern Show* was the highest-rated syndicated radio show in the country. Stern continued to amuse and amaze his loyal following while reaching a new generation of listeners with his timeless brand of reality radio. His penchant for anything raunchy or disgusting, for taking shots at whomever he did not like (especially the FCC), and for being very candid about his own life never seemed to grow old.

Success breeds imitators with a hit TV or radio show. By the late 1990s there were Stern imitators on radio stations all over the country. They were not trying to imitate Stern's program specifically, but they were trying to cash in on his radio style, stream of consciousness humor, racy and suggestive content, and outrageous games and comedy bits. Yet few could compete with Howard Stern just being Howard Stern and his simple concept of being honest, vulnerable, and talking about himself. He found humor in simple things like describing his brief career in art where he found himself in a class full of artists and had no idea what he was doing. Nonetheless, it has been said that "Imitation is the greatest form of flattery," since you need to be doing something very well for people to want to imitate what you do. Whether he liked the imitators or not, Stern must have been flattered by all those trying to duplicate his style.

THE 9/11 ATTACKS

It was a typical September morning in 2001, and Stern and the gang were talking about Pamela Anderson, a favorite topic at the time, when they were interrupted by the news of an airplane crashing into the World Trade Center in lower Manhattan. As was the case with most radio programs, the news came in slowly as reporters raced to the scene. At first, Stern and company could only surmise what had happened. Before they could return to the subject at hand, a second plane had struck the other World Trade Center tower, and it was clear that the earlier crash was no accident. For the first time in modern history the United States mainland was under attack.

Stern remained on air for his full show, broadcasting during the tragedy that was September 11, 2001. While Stern joked that suddenly he was doing the job of acclaimed newscaster Dan Rather, he was trying diligently to figure out what was going on, along with most people. While Stern was trying hard, the show drew some criticism because glib comments in the early morning from Robin Quivers, that we should go out and attack someone, were misguided when people were in peril just a few miles away. This was a time to report on the people in need of rescue, the loved ones of those listening, the efforts of the police and the fire department, not yet the time to respond with an attack. People were scared, not yet ready to stage a war, but fearing for their safety. Yes, Stern was among the first to name Bin Laden as the man most likely behind this, and yes the United States did need to go after him, but events of that morning were all about what was happening at the World Trade Center and what people needed to know about the immediate tragedy. Racist callers, with their skewed viewpoints of the world, like the one who said, "Run all the towel heads out of the country," were totally out of place at that moment. Another caller still wanted to talk about Pamela Anderson, but Stern quickly dismissed him. The situation was too big and the need for real information was too great. Stern had not been trained to handle a major crisis, and even many seasoned news reporters were not completely sure what to do with a major tragedy of this magnitude, unfolding as they spoke. Although Stern deserves a lot of credit for staying on the air and trying to handle the situation, he (not unlike many seasoned broadcasters) was not trained to handle a major crisis, and the radio station should not have put him in the situation when they could have been switching back and forth to their news division for more comprehensive reporting of the events taking place. In subsequent days, like other comedy programs, the show took on an appropriately somber tone, and Stern and the gang dealt very well with the ongoing situation while the country remained in shock. Robin Quivers would later take heat for commenting that the people on the planes were cowards for not trying to fight back, as was the case with the one flight that crashed in Pennsylvania. Not being in such a situation and having no idea what happened on those tragic flights makes it awfully hard for Quivers, or anyone else, to criticize the victims of such a tragedy.

ENTER ARTIE LANGE

In late October 2001, the show finally ushered in a replacement for Jackie Martling, who had left over a contract dispute earlier in March 2001. The choice was Artie Lange, who had been one of many guest comics over the previous months as the show searched for a full-time replacement for Martling.

Lange's road to the Stern show was a rollercoaster ride. He grew up in a middle-class Italian family in Union, New Jersey, helping his dad with contracting jobs and playing baseball for his high school team. He was good enough, at baseball to be named All County at third base. Lange planned to go to college, but his plans changed abruptly when his father fell from a roof and was paralyzed. Lange needed to help support his family, so he took on various jobs, eventually becoming a longshoreman at the docks in Newark, New Jersey.

Lange always had a skewed look at the world and a very sharp comic mind, so he started performing stand-up comedy and working with improvisational troupes in and around New York City. In 1995, the producers of Mad TV, the new Fox TV sketch comedy program, saw one of his improvisational performances and invited him to join the cast.

Show business took its toll on Lange, however, and a substance abuse problem and an arrest for cocaine possession led to Lange being fired from Mad TV in 1997. After a stint in rehab, Lange found himself looking for work in Los Angeles.

A comic friend, Norm Macdonald, remembered Lange and cast him in his 1998 movie *Dirty Work,* a comedy directed by Bob Saget about a business that specialized in getting revenge for those who wanted, or needed, it. The movie did not generate many good reviews or big bucks, but it led to a regular role for Lange on Macdonald's sitcom, *The Norm Show.* For Lange it was steady work with great pay.

While working on *The Norm Show* (which ended in 2001), Lange continued to perform stand-up comedy, and returned to drug abuse. By the time he joined *The Howard Stern Show,* he was a top-notch, highly paid comic with plenty of baggage, including drugs, drinking, overeating, gambling, and frequenting prostitutes. Despite generating big laughs on stage, Lange was insecure and had nothing stable in his life to keep him grounded. He did have two very redeeming qualities: he was extremely funny and was a long-time listener and fan of *The Howard Stern Show*. Thus, Lange fit right in when Stern or anyone else would make references to previous shows, regular guests, or frequent callers.

Although Lange could be as crass as any of the Stern regulars, in contrast to Martling, he also brought a smarter brand of comedy to the show, making quips about anything from show staffers to politics or newsworthy events. Lange had greater versatility than Marling whose repertoire, while very funny, was limited. Lange's humor is often dry or cynical but very sharp. He will often hit the nail on the head without the need for an obvious punch line, such as the time Stern was talking on the phone with Daniel Carver, a regular caller and occasional guest who is the former grand leader of the Ku Klux Klan. Stern typically let Carver spew his racist, anti-Semitic, and caustic remarks without interjecting humor, allowing listeners to take from Carver's comments what they will. On one particular occasion, while Carver was rambling about his dislike of Barack Obama as an African American president, the subject of who could join the Ku Klux Klan came up. Obviously, Stern, being Jewish, and Quivers, being African American, would be excluded from the racist group. When Lange asked whether he would be accepted, Carver said he thought Lange drank too much. At this Lange exclaimed indignantly, "I can see why you don't want a black or a Jew, but a guy who drinks a lot? I thought that was all you guys did."[1]

In addition to adding his sharp wit to the show, Lange proved to be a challenge to Stern and the show's cast as they tried to keep him on the show and out of trouble. Over the years, Lange dozed off during the show on several occasions and was quite drunk during an on-location broadcast from Las Vegas. He has missed work on several occasions, once because he returned to his previous heroin habit. Lange has discussed on air the agonizing time of going through heroin withdrawal. He is now on prescribed medication that has helped him to stay clean from the dangerous drug.

The Artie Lange story is an ongoing soap opera that fits well in the world of Stern and his on-air family. Unlike Quivers, Norris, and Dell'Abate, whose careers center primarily on the show, Lange maintains his stand-up comedy career, bringing in top dollar for shows around the country. His tales from the road, his vulnerability, and his perpetual bad, sometimes dangerous, habits make for very real reality radio—which is what *The Howard Stern Show* is all about.

EXIT ALISON

One of the most challenging times for Howard Stern was in 2001, when he and Alison, his wife of more than 20 years, ended their marriage. News of the separation and impending divorce came as a shock to Stern fans who felt as if Alison was part of their family, because they knew so much about her through Stern's on-air descriptions of their life together. Alison had stuck with Stern through the difficult early years and had convinced him that his foray into advertising was not the way to go. It was Alison who understood better than anyone else what her husband was trying to accomplish and recognized that the strippers, porn stars, and other women who clamored to be on the radio show were all part of the Stern radio world. Stern swore time and time again, on air, that he had always been faithful to Alison, and those who knew him, believed him, because Stern was, if nothing else, honest.

Together they had three daughters, raised primarily by Alison because of Stern's difficult schedule. The divorce was largely because, after so many years together, Alison had grown tired of being the second love of Howard Stern's life, behind the radio show. She knew he was faithful, a good person, and a good father, and although she did not fault him for his passion and commitment to being the best at what he did, she wanted more of his time and devotion. By the end of the 1990s, financially Stern could have easily walked away from radio at the end of his contract. He had accumulated millions of dollars from the radio show, books, movies, television show, and other sources, and the Sterns were quite affluent and set for life. Yet, although Stern loved Alison and wanted to be there more often for his daughters, he was a workaholic, self-admittedly obsessed with his career. Painful as it was, the divorce was amicable and mutual. Alison walked away with a great deal of money and custody of their three daughters. Stern made it clear that if he was ever needed to take custody or be there in any way for his girls, he would do so.

Shortly after the divorce was official, Alison announced that she was marrying David Simon, CEO of shopping mall giant Simon Property Group. The two were married in late 2001. Stern was happy for her, yet rather surprised that she would jump into a second marriage so soon after their 23 years together. Nonetheless, he sat with his daughters and kept a low profile at Alison's wedding.

Meanwhile, Stern also made a major commitment—therapy four days a week. After the divorce, Stern admitted on air and in interviews that he wished he'd been a better parent. He loved his daughters, but because of his workaholic ways didn't feel that he had been able to get as close to them as he would have liked. He also revealed during interviews at that time, that he was in denial about the marital problems with Alison and was not able to see that his career was taking its toll on their marriage. "It's sad that it ended. It still pains me," Stern was quoted as saying after the divorce.[2]

Clearly, the divorce was a painful time for Stern, yet he could not let it detract from the tone of the show. Through it all, he continued to produce quality radio while still focusing on the well-being of his daughters. Gossip columnists were eager for stories, but Stern, as always, kept his family away from the media circus.

SINGLE AGAIN

Stern was once again single, only now much richer and more famous than in his pre-Alison, gawky, dateless days. He took an apartment in Manhattan overlooking Central Park. Stern could now make some of the fantasies he discussed on-air come true. He started by dating supermodel Angie Everhart and then ex-Baywatch star Carmen Electra. However, it wasn't very long before he found himself involved in another relationship, this time with swimsuit model Beth Ostrosky. They had met at a dinner party, hit it off, and started dating. After several months, Stern brought the news to his listeners that he and Beth were indeed an item, although the press was already following their every move in public.

Born in 1972, in Pittsburgh, Pennsylvania, Beth is nearly 18 years younger than Stern. Beth had started a modeling career at the age of nine, spurred on by her mom, who had also been a model. Beth O., as she would later become known, did some commercials in Pennsylvania and then made her way to New York City, where she was a natural for modeling jobs (her height, 5'10" to Stern's 6'4," contributed to her success). By the late 1990s, she had become best known for her swimsuit modeling. Like many models, Beth wanted to expand her career and move into acting, which she did in the Ben Stiller movie *Flirting with Disaster* and the Amanda Peet film *Whipped*.

Once the relationship went public, Ostrosky's life changed, and she was constantly in the public eye. Photo shoots, interviews, and acting roles increased, and Beth O. became a modest celebrity, despite her claims to the contrary. Yet she still tried to stay out of the media frenzy and away from the paparazzi, letting Stern do the talking and deal with the hordes of reporters and photographers that met them nearly every place they went.

Although he continued to admit that radio came first in his life, Stern was also conscious of not making the same mistake twice and tried hard to make sufficient time for Beth and for his daughters. Fortunately, Beth and Stern's three girls got along well. Within a short time, Beth moved in with Stern at his Manhattan apartment. They also spent time at Stern's summer home in the Hamptons, an exclusive area of Long Island where the rich play and party during the warmer months.

The new relationship was not the only significant change in Howard Stern's life. In the early 2000s, the emergence of satellite radio would be the next major stepping stone for Howard Stern, his radio family, and his listeners. He would soon become the face of this new medium.

THE EMERGENCE OF SATELLITE RADIO

In 1992, when Stern was just beginning to emerge as a star of syndicated radio, reaching new markets around the country one by one, the FCC was establishing the Digital Audio Radio Service (DARS). All radio stations are transmitted over specific frequencies, and DARS consisted of frequencies that were being set aside for satellite broadcasting on radio. Television had started broadcasting via satellite in March 1978, and by the advent of satellite radio in 1992, all major television networks had been using satellites to broadcast to local television stations (known as affiliates) for several years.

Satellite led to innovations in radio. Unlike television, where the major broadcast networks had local affiliates nationwide, most radio stations, even those owned by large conglomerates, were independent and had their own programming. Running an independent local radio station cost a fraction of what it cost to run a television station. Along with far less expensive equipment (i.e., lights and cameras) it was much easier to program a local radio station. All you needed was someone behind a microphone plus some music, ads, and sound effects at the ready.

Radio syndication brought the first changes, and syndicated shows such as *The Howard Stern Show* began to reach several different markets. Still, the industry could not compare to the wide-reaching television networks, where you could find your favorite network program in almost any town, city, or county coast to coast. Satellite was envisioned as the first step toward national radio stations.

The new frequencies that had been set aside were auctioned to companies that believed they could provide such national radio networks. American Mobile Radio (which would become XM radio) bought its license for $93 million and CD Radio (which would become Sirius Satellite Radio) purchased its license for $89 million. In addition to the money for licenses and the frequencies, building a satellite radio network cost billions of dollars.

By 2000, there was a buzz about subscriber satellite radio. The question was whether or not people would pay for radio and what they would get for their money that they couldn't get from traditional AM and FM radio stations.

It wasn't long before XM launched its first two broadcast satellites, Rock (March 18, 2001) and Roll (May 8, 2001), which in a short time were available throughout the country. Sirius radio followed shortly thereafter, launching in several markets (in 2002). Some people immediately got onboard, purchasing the equipment and signing up as subscribers. Many others, however, didn't really want to pay for radio, especially when frequencies could still be subject to interference by tall buildings and trees.

One positive aspect of the new medium was that for a monthly payment, listeners were no longer subjected to numerous commercials. In addition, there were more niche markets than could be found on AM and FM radio, such as various types of country music or rock stations. Sports fans could now tune into games other than those of their local teams. Another feature was that, like pay television, censorship was much looser. Those who wanted uninterrupted music, sports, or talk radio were happier to buy the equipment and pay the monthly fees. By 2002, car manufacturers were installing satellite radio receivers in most new automobiles.

The biggest news in satellite radio occurred in 2004, when Sirius offered Stern a five-year contract for $500 million. Needless to say, Stern accepted the offer. How could he not? This was by far the most lucrative radio contract ever, exceeding the total value or sale of most radio stations throughout the United States.

THE WINDFALL DEAL

Only football fans remember who won the 2003 Super Bowl, but nearly everyone recalls the infamous Janet Jackson "wardrobe malfunction" in which, for a fleeting second, one of her breasts was revealed during the halftime show. The incident became a major news story resulting in huge fines against the halftime show organizers. The incident also sent the FCC on a rampage, cracking down on anything and everything that could be perceived as offensive. In fact, the FCC enacted a zero-tolerance policy toward indecency shortly after the Janet Jackson incident. Stern was among the first targets, and heavy fines ensued along with suspension by Clear Channel Communications (the parent company behind the Stern show) in six different markets after Stern had an on-air, in-depth conversation with Paris Hilton's ex-boyfriend, Rick Salomon, about their personal life.

In 2003, the presidential campaign was also under way between President George W. Bush and the Democratic challenger, Senator John Kerry. Stern, who had been a supporter of George W. Bush in the 2000 campaign had lost faith in him and had become a firm supporter of Senator Kerry. Stern was very outspoken about politics, bashing Bush for the mismanaged war in Iraq among other issues. Although much of Stern's audience was not a heavily politically minded group, his message to vote for Kerry was reaching millions of listeners. Although unproven, Stern, among others, believed his political views resulted in extra scrutiny by the FCC, which was headed by the son of Colin Powell, who was, like Bush, a Republican (Howard Stern Confronts FCC Chairman in Talkradio Showdown, http://www.democraticunderground.com/discuss/duboard.php?az=view_all&address=104x2542388). If you recall from the preface, the Smothers Brothers ran up against censorship largely because President Richard Nixon did not want to be criticized. The point being that Stern's theories may not have been that far fetched.

In addition to the lucrative contract, the Sirius offer appealed to Stern's desire to get away from the fines and constant scrutiny that came with being on AM or FM radio. In some of the many interviews that followed the bombshell announcement of his signing with Sirius Satellite Radio, he stated that the move was largely a response to the endless censorship battles with the FCC. He would finally be able to do his show as he wanted, without being under the FCC's microscope. Stern had stated that he was losing his passion for radio because of the constant battles, and he was also disappointed that Clear Channel Communications did not put up more of a fight on his behalf. After all, he was a leading source of revenue.

For Sirius, making such a record-breaking financial offer was a huge financial gamble. Could Stern bring in enough of his fans to raise their subscriber base from 600,000 to several million? That's what it would take to cover Stern's salary and actually turn a profit. The thinking, however, was to legitimize the new satellite radio by bringing in the biggest name in the industry. It was also thought that if Stern made the move to satellite radio other top radio personalities would follow.

Only time would tell, as the deal was set to commence in January 2006. It gave Sirius plenty of time to roll out a major promotional campaign in advance of Stern's impending arrival and to sell subscriptions. Although some of Stern's long-time loyal following would resist paying to hear their hero, the hope was that many would appreciate the fact that censorship rules were now lifted and Stern could do his show without the constant worry that "big brother" was watching.

As anticipated, subscriptions rose rapidly after Sirius announced that Stern would soon be on board. For Stern it was now only a matter of time before he would rid himself of the shackles of censorship. But what would that mean for Stern's program? Without fighting the FCC and station personnel, would Stern have the same edginess? That became the question many Stern followers, both fans and critics, debated as his satellite radio debut drew near. Part of the appeal of *The Howard Stern Show* was listening to his reactions to the latest trouble he was in and the latest fines the FCC levied on his employers. Ratings soared on the days after stories broke in the newspapers about Stern being in trouble. Everyone wanted to see what happened, and Stern didn't disappoint, lambasting all those who were complaining about his latest on-air antics. Without a nemesis, would Stern still be as fascinating? Stern made it clear on interview after interview that the new show would be funnier because it would be uncensored.

Meanwhile, as Stern began preparing for the switch to satellite radio, executives at K-Rock and Clear Channel were trying to figure out how to replace him. It was later revealed that Gary Dell'Abate and Artie Lange were offered a deal to do their own show, but turned it down to stay with Howard Stern. The mutual respect, not to mention the paychecks, was part of what kept the Stern radio family together and would keep them intact for the move to satellite radio.

TELEVISION CHANGES ALSO BREWING

News of Stern's deal was everywhere. It was a landmark media deal financially and a coup for the young satellite radio network. Stern had earned money for radio stations everywhere he went and had built a huge following. There was no reason to doubt that he could launch Sirius to great heights.

The news, however, was not welcomed by the E! network. In fact, the new radio deal put the long-running Howard Stern E! television show in jeopardy. The already censored version of the television show would now need to be censored for verbal content and visual images. Concerned that the editing process would all but eliminate the program entirely, E! canceled the show and proceeded to air the 2,000 episodes in reruns until the contract expired.

Stern, however, wanted to continue a television version of the radio program as it had been a hit on E! for more than a decade. The most logical option for Stern would be to take the television version of the radio program to HBO or Showtime, the leading pay channels on cable. Such channels have no outside advertising and face minimal censorship.

THE CABLE AND SATELLITE CENSORSHIP BATTLE

As mentioned earlier, since the emergence of pay television in the 1970s, there have been long-running debates over censorship issues. As channels such as HBO and Showtime, among others, have become more readily available in households and even hotels all over the country (and worldwide), concern about the accessibility of uncensored programming to minors has grown. Nudity, sexual content, extreme violence, illegal drug use, and inappropriate language, issues that still concern parents, have sparked some of the outcry for greater censorship. In sharp contrast to free network television and radio, where first amendment battles for freedom of speech have resulted in fines, firings, and protests, freedom of speech and free expression have been welcomed in this new cable (and satellite) world. Yet, even those with the most vocal arguments against censorship agree with the need to keep children from watching and listening to inappropriate material. They believe, however, that the burden should be on the parents not the networks. Rather than telling HBO, Showtime, or Sirius Radio what they can and cannot offer the public, supporters of less censorship believe that responsible parents need to control what their children watch on television and even what they listen to on the radio. Those supporting such freedom of speech and lack of censorship argue that, if you bring alcohol, prescription medications, tools, sharp objects, or even a gun into your home, it is not the manufacturer's responsibility to see that your child does not use such items, but your responsibility as a parent.

The counter argument is that such uncensored programming is too easy to access. No matter how hard parents try to monitor what their children watch and listen to, the sheer volume of such material makes it impossible to keep it away from minors. Even commercials and sound bites can be inappropriate, and it becomes near to impossible to control what a child comes in contact with during the course of any given day. The battle over censorship continues, with some valid claims on both sides of the debate

TV SAYS NO TO STERN

Much to Stern's surprise, HBO turned him down, as did the other major cable outlets, leaving only a few logical choices, such as Spike TV (which showed interest in 2005 but never presented a deal), which is largely geared to his young male audience. Spike, however, is a basic cable channel and not an individual pay channel, meaning there would still need to be heavy editing of the uncensored Sirius programs. In addition, Spike had a small viewing audience, and some local cable affiliates did not carry the fairly new channel. It would take some major promotion to get viewers to find the channel at all. In time, Stern decided that the only way to succeed in bringing his brand of uncensored reality/comedic programming to television would be to do it all himself, with his own pay network, which will be explored in the next chapter.

THE UNCENSORED SHOW BEGINS

On January 9, 2006, in a larger studio than ever before, Howard Stern, Robin Quivers, Artie Lange, Fred Norris, Gay Dell'Abate and an extended crew launched the long awaited, much anticipated, uncensored *Howard Stern Show* on Sirius Satellite Radio, Channel 100. There was plenty of hype, many promotional interviews, and lots of media coverage. An estimated one million listeners tuned in, which was about ten percent of the size of his previous syndicated audience.

After the long wait, Stern's highly anticipated debut on this new media outlet was interrupted early on by technical difficulties with telephone and microphone links, forcing Stern to do what he had moved away from so many years before—play music. However, within a short time, the technical glitches were resolved, and the first show was under way. Within minutes, it was Howard Stern being Howard Stern, talking off the cuff about his personal life along with the news items of the day. Little had changed except that Stern and company could curse freely (the *USA Today* review of the show counted 172 profanities from

Stern and the crew in the 4 hours of air time, or 43 profanities per hour).

A new on-air game called Revelations featured personal revelations by members of the Howard Stern radio family, such as one crew member who was caught cheating on his wife or another who had his stomach pumped for alcohol poisoning. The audience tried to guess which revelation belonged to which crew member. One of the early guests to the show, George Takei, a cast member from the original *Star Trek*, had come out of the closet only a few months earlier, stating that he was gay. Like all guests and all of Stern's cast and crew, Takei was subjected to the usual barbs. No one was safe and nothing was off limits, which made it acceptable to make fun of anyone and made guests feel accepted into the world of Howard Stern. In a society in which there is a tremendous emphasis on political correctness, one of the hallmarks of the *Howard Stern Show* has always been to speak openly and honestly about all races, creeds, colors, religions, and nationalities. Stern was always the first to indulge in self-deprecation, putting down himself, his parents, his upbringing, and anything else from his own life that he felt didn't measure up.

Takei was a fan of the show and had been making guest appearances for some 15 years. Although his role as an on-air announcer was minimal, he brought the show some new perspectives. Along with a gay and Asian perspective, Takei had years of experiences from a film career that began long before *Star Trek* had immortalized him as Sulu. The 72-year-old actor had appeared in major films with John Wayne, Richard Burton, Jerry Lewis, Cary Grant, and other screen legends before ever meeting William Shatner as Captain Kirk on *Star Trek*. He also brought along his own dry wit. Takei continues to sit in with the Stern crew for a week every few months.

After the initial broadcast, the hoopla died down, and Stern was once again doing what he does best, filling hours of radio time each morning with a mix of crude, rude, unabashed, and now uncensored insights into virtually anywhere his mind took him, plus the usual games, guests, and a variety of well-planned segments.

As Sirius had invested a fortune into *The Howard Stern Show*, the company was determined to get the most for its buck by replaying the show throughout the day, enabling them to draw new Stern listeners who could not listen in the morning hours. The fact that the show was done during the morning did not factor heavily into the content or success of the show. Unlike local DJs, who were busy catching up morning commuters on the weather and traffic, Stern was far removed from such updates, and the show had no real connection with the morning hours, other than Lange falling asleep on occasion during a broadcast. Taping the syndicated show in the morning allowed Stern to get the upper hand when trying to prompt his studio guests and phone callers to reveal personal details. After all, although Stern was wide eyed and at his best at 6 A.M., many of his guests had not yet had their morning coffee and were looser lipped than they might have been with a whole day to craft their answers.

THE GUEST LIST

The guest list had grown over the years, and by the time Stern moved to Sirius it included many A-list celebrities who knew the promotional power of appearing on Stern's show. Paul McCartney, Chris Rock, Jamie Foxx, AC/DC, 50 Cent, Seth Rogan, Jimmy Fallon, Ben Stiller, Jimmy Kimmel, Jon Bon Jovi, Drew Carey, Joan Rivers, Ben Affleck, Jennifer Lopez, Alec Baldwin, Bill Maher, Johnny Depp, Denise Richards, Jerry Seinfeld, Bob Saget, Chevy Chase, Cindy Crawford, Ringo Starr, Sandra Bullock, Don Rickles, Donald Trump, and Ron Howard are just a few of the major name stars that have dared sit in the hot seat with Howard Stern.

Stern also continued trying to get the sexiest female stars to appear on the show. Carmen Electra and Pamela Anderson were among the hot A-listers who dodged personal questions while promoting their latest shows, tapes, books, or films. Although Stern remains respectful of the more significant guests (while still asking probing questions) he has always been able to take a looser approach with offbeat guests, hasbeens, porn stars, strippers, and sexy models.

Sometimes the guests can be extremely funny and, in other cases, very temperamental, such as when Stern had Amy Fisher on the program. As a teenager, Fisher made the headlines after shooting (but not killing) the wife of her much older boyfriend, Joey Buttafuoco. After spending time in jail, Fisher and Buttafuoco made sensual videos, which Fisher was promoting on the air. When Stern took a phone call from the daughter of the woman she had shot, Fisher got up and left the studio, saying she would not go through any more on the subject, having served her time in jail.

On other shows, such as the one with actor Jeff Conaway, of television series *Taxi* and the movie *Grease*, the interview delved into some very serious matters, such as Conaway's painful years of extreme drug addiction and rehabilitation and his victimization by child pornographers when he was a youth. Conway's career had spiraled downhill and he told his painful story to Stern.

Sometimes Stern simply couldn't stand the guest, or at least the way he or she was acting. One rule for going on *The Howard Stern Show* has always been that you are expected to be yourself. He has always lost his patience with guests who are putting on an act. Back in the mid-1990s, for example, he had made it clear to comedienne Rhonda Sheer and her cohort, who visited the show to promote a cable TV program, that he couldn't stand them and that they were annoying because they kept on doing shtick, playing for the audience, and aggravating him. Typically, Stern and company try to see how far an annoying guest is willing to go to stay on the program. In this particular instance, in what has become one of the classic guest moments, Sheer agreed to let him strap her into the famous tickle chair. However, while Stern was tickling her, Sheer broke the second rule of going on *The Howard Stern Show*: do not injure the host. While Stern was leaning over her, she bit down hard on his long hair and pulled some of his hair out. Stern was both shocked and in pain. Needless to say, he wasn't happy and Sheer was quickly asked to exit the studio.

From program to program and guest to guest anything can happen, and Stern has tapes of all sorts of offbeat incidents and investigative conversations to prove it. There is no pattern or prepared scripted interactions as is the case with many other talk shows, which is what has made Stern's reality radio show so successful. The move to Sirius has also allowed guests to speak freely if they want to, which for some of the edgier comics, is much appreciated.

JUST WHEN HE THOUGHT IT WAS OVER

With the FCC and the censorship watchdogs off his back, one might assume that Howard Stern would get a long awaited rest from radio warfare. However, peace and prosperity didn't last very long. Just over one month into the new Sirius Satellite Radio contract, Stern, along with his long-time agent, Don Buchwald, were sued by CBS Radio, his previous employer, for promoting his upcoming Sirius show while on the CBS (K-Rock) airwaves. The lawsuit, which included 43 pages of complaint charges, also focused on some $200 million in stock Sirius gave to Stern for helping it top its anticipated subscriber numbers even before he hit the airwaves. CBS contended that Stern was using its airwaves to advertise and promote the upcoming Sirius radio program, while the satellite network was not paying for the advertising time. In addition, by promoting Sirius Satellite Radio, Stern was bringing the stock price up, again while on CBS radio. As a result, the lawsuit was for compensatory and punitive damages for breach of contract, fraud, and misappropriation of CBS radio's broadcast time.

In response to the lawsuit, Stern pointed out that in the final months before he moved to Sirius Satellite Radio, CBS booked him on *Late Night with David Letterman* and used the impending contract news to promote Stern's show. He also reminded CBS that if he had been doing something wrong, they had had the right at any time to pull the plug on his show and take him off the air. Stern claimed that they didn't do anything because he was still bringing in big bucks for the CBS network.[3]

By the spring, a settlement was reached between CBS, Stern, and Sirius. Exactly how much money changed hands in the settlement was not known. However, one thing Sirius did get was 23,000 hours of Howard Stern's radio shows to use if they so chose for the five years of their contract. After that time ownership of the shows would revert to Stern himself. Maintaining creative control over content has always been important to Stern, and using good business sense, he always kept up with ownership rights to his radio programs and the subsequent television versions.

SOMETHING FOR THE FANS: THE HOWARD STERN FILM FESTIVAL

In 2006, Howard Stern decided it was high time to take on another project. However, this was a behind-the-scenes and promotional endeavor in the form of a film festival featuring short movies made by his loyal following about the King of All Media himself.

With $25,000 and other prizes for the top films, the festival began in New York City. The films were not expected to be of the quality of major film festivals like those at Cannes or Sundance. These would be Howard Stern–themed, outrageous, amateur efforts, many of which would probably have been rejected from *America's Funniest Home Videos*. Quality notwithstanding, a film critic from the *Chicago Sun Times*, Richard Roeper; director Todd Phillips of the films *Old School* and *Starsky & Hutch*; and Richard Belzer, a comic and costar of television's *Law and Order: SVU* agreed to be judges.

Films had to be under five minutes as anything longer might be considered cruel and unusual punishment. More than 2,000 entries came pouring in, and, indeed, they were unusual. The Stern staff brought in extra screeners to weed through the many entries and narrow it down to the best of the worst.

The festival was primarily a very clever means of promoting the Sirius radio program and Stern's new on-demand television deal. It was also a way to let the fans share in their love of their hero by depicting him on film—and they did by donning all sorts of long-haired wigs and trying in vain to act.

In the end, the final awards were given out at a red carpet affair at the Hudson Theater in Times Square. Along with Stern's crew, many of the odd characters who had made regular appearances on the program over the years (known as the Wack Pack) were on hand, along with a few of the competing filmmakers whose work was deemed better than the rest.

Because the festival took place at the same time as actor Robert DeNiro's popular New York Tribeca Film Festival, comparisons were made. When asked about the comparison to the Tribeca Film Festival, Artie Lange had the most appropriate comparison. He stated quite simply, "Our films suck."

In the end, nine entries were featured at the Hudson Theater event. Featuring flatulence and other bodily functions, crude jokes, and tasteless gags, the films served as an appropriate crude, lewd, and rude tribute to Stern from his adoring fans. Ironically, the film that won the grand prize was not crass or tasteless at all, but somewhat touching in its tribute to Stern and his cohorts. The film, called *Radio Days*, by David Scott Masterson, an aspiring young filmmaker from Massachusetts, was a look back at childhood versions of Howard Stern, Robin Quivers, and Fred Norris as if they had met many years earlier. It was oddly touching, clever, and clearly of a higher quality than the rest of the entries.[4]

The film festival was successful on many other measures as it drew fans into the world of their hero, while promoting the Sirius show, which had far surpassed the one million fan subscriber goal, reaching 3.5 million within a few months of Stern's arrival. The additional 2.5 million subscribers earned Stern a bonus of $83 million for his first anniversary from the very generous folks at Sirius.

The festival was also an excellent way of promoting the new television venture, HTV, or Howard Television, which would finally provide the same uncensored versions of the radio show on pay television. With his own television network and a production company to boot, Stern had successfully ventured into all media, with the possible exception of a Broadway show.

THE MERGER

In the summer of 2008, Sirius and XM, the two competing satellite radio giants, merged and became Sirius XM Radio Inc. Sirius had been winning the competition in a major way, largely thanks to the draw of Howard Stern. This allowed them to purchase XM Satellite Radio. As a result, the merger pooled the subscribers of the two networks. Now there were more than 18.5 million potential listeners to *The Howard Stern Show*. At $12.95 per month, that's $2.8+ billion in annual revenue, making it easy to pay Stern his $100 million annual salary through 2010. The merger did not affect Howard Stern's programming, but it did broaden his listening audience.

COMPETITION? WHAT COMPETITION?

Stern always faced competition on terrestrial radio, but he has faced perhaps his toughest competitors since his move to Sirius: Greg Hughes and Anthony Cumia, better known as the hosts of the *Opie & Anthony Show*, which airs on satellite radio during the same morning hours as *The Howard Stern Show*. Clearly influenced by Stern, the duo first grew to great popularity in Massachusetts and then, like Stern, on WXRK-FM in New York (formerly known as K-Rock), from which they were let go in early 2009 when the long-time rock station switched formats to Top 40. Opie and Anthony's shock jock style has prompted several online discussion boards in which their loyal listeners have challenged Stern listeners, proclaiming that their heroes are hotter and funnier than Stern, while Stern's faithful have responded as only they can by blasting the new team.

The duo was formed in 1995, shortly after Cumia took part in an impression contest on *The Howard Stern Show*. Cumia not only imitated Jackie the Jokeman but also Beavis and Butthead. While Opie and Anthony are not quite the household names Howard Stern has become, nor have they built a following through reality radio, they certainly have raised the bar on shock value, starting with an April Fool's Day joke where they told everyone on air that the mayor of Boston had been killed in a car accident. The mayor's daughter happened to be listening and called the station horrified, believing it to be true, only to learn that it was a sick joke. The incident got the duo fired, which they claimed is what they were going for.[5]

On a lighter note, they held a contest for people to have sex in public places, which led to several arrests. This, along with various other stunts, some of which have led to suspensions, even from Sirius, have brought them notoriety. Yet the comic duo still does not generate the mass media attention, have the legions of long-time fans, or have their own television network as does Howard Stern. The next chapter will explore HTV.

NOTES

1. *The Howard Stern Show*. Sirius Radio, January 23, 2009.

2. The Complete Howard Stern Links! Web site. A Brief Howard Stern Bio. Available at: http://www.animaux.net/stern/bio.

3. Corey Deitz, "CBS Radio Sues Howard Stern, His Company, His Agent and SIRIUS Satellite Radio," February 28, 2006. http://radio.about.com/od/howardstern/a/aa022806.htm.

4. Howard Stern film festival press releases, April 2006. "Winner of Howard Stern Film Festival Is a Shocker" by Robert Mancini at MTV.com. http://www.mtv.com/movies/news/articles/1529773/20060428/story.jhtml.

5. "Joke May Be on Shock Jocks," by Fernanda Santos, *Daily News*, August 17, 2002. Available at: http://www.nydailynews.com/archives/news/2002/08/17/2002-08-17_joke_may_be_on_shock_jocks.html.

Chapter 5

HOWARD TV, THE WOMEN IN STERN'S WORLD, AND THE CELEBRITY WEDDING

The categories were updated to keep fresh programming available. Excerpts from the daily shows would be added each week. The content could now be selected by the Stern staff to show the best and most visually enticing moments of the weekly shows.

Stern had a greater say in what would air on HTV and a say in who would handle each of the many new jobs. He needed to have a top-notch television crew in place to produce the show and solve problems that arose in getting the shows on the air. The objective was to enable Stern to stay out of the technical mix and focus his energies on the content and the entertainment value, as he had always done on radio.

GOOD TELEVISION

Putting a radio program on television doesn't immediately sound particularly appealing to the viewer. After all, watching the people sitting at microphones doesn't sound very exciting. Stern, however, had long made it a point of having more visual entertainment on his program (often in the way of sexy women) and for years had described the game shows and various in-studio activities to his audience. The uncensored versions of all of this, along with uncensored celebrity interviews, would make for great programming. As a visual medium, HTV could do one more important thing for its viewers: show the Howard Stern family and their interactions on a regular basis. Lange, Quivers, Norris, Dell'Abate, and a host of others, as well as the off-beat characters that make up the Wack Pack, would now become that much more real and familiar to viewers with regular television exposure. Despite his radio background, Stern knew what made up a good television show, and with this new venture was he very careful to maintain the high production quality that he had always insisted upon for his fans.

HTV: THE CATEGORIES

From the 4-hour daily radio show, Stern pulled out the segments that were most likely to draw viewers. And to make programming easy for subscribers to find, a menu of categories was established. Stern and the staff sorted the raunchy from the raunchier to provide a number of choices to keep viewers coming back month after month. So, along with the daily shows, the HTV menu featured the following categories:

- *The Vault*: Here, viewers could look at selected programs from years ago, featuring interviews, episodes from the infamous Stern Show trip to Las Vegas, comedy roasts of cast members or other celebrities and other classic moments from years gone by.
- *Favorite Guests*: This category offered segments of the best guests who had sat in for Stern interviews over the years.
- *Girls Girls Girls*: It wouldn't be *The Howard Stern Show* without sexy female guests. This category included interviews and racy segments with some of the many women who have visited the show.
- *Sexy Fun & Games*: From Win Fred's Money to plenty of other games with sexy consequences, this is where the viewers could watch some of the games and bits that Stern has, for so many years, described to his listening audience.
- *Wacky & Weird*: This features all of the outrageous activities and stunts that go on during the show. Quirky games, strange contests, and bits that have no other classification fall under Wacky & Weird.
- *Fan Favorites*: This category is for the episodes fans most want to see again and again.
- *Wrap-Up Shows*: Here, fans get a behind-the-scenes look at wrap-up meetings, which provides a glimpse into what happens after the daily radio shows conclude. These wrap-up sessions are where the crew, led by producer Gary Dell'Abate, discuss, debate, and argue over what could have been done better and what worked well. For years the wrap-up meetings have been an important part of the daily show production, but only recently have they become something fans could watch.

• *Original Programming*: To supplement content from the radio programs, the network added original programming that ranged from the entertaining and quirky to the bad and unwatchable. These included *Bowling Beauties*, which featured women bowling in bikinis, and *Strip Beer Pong*. Ronnie Mund, Howard Stern's limo driver and bodyguard, was given his own show, and Richard Christie took viewers to his family farm along with an angry clown, a porn star, and a mentally handicapped member of the Wack Pack in a show that was a dysfunctional reality version of *Green Acres*. The offbeat original shows that pop up on HTV give the cast and crew their moments in the limelight and build the notoriety of the world of Howard Stern.

MISS HOWARD TV

Before the emergence of HTV, there were a few Miss Howard Sterns. One was the winner of the infamous New Year's Rotten Eve beauty contest, while another, Andrea Ownbey, earned the title during the show's trip to Las Vegas. The new network, however, needed someone to introduce each month's programs in a short promotional segment, and that became the monthly Miss Howard TV.

Whether she was discovered by a cast or crew member, sent photos to the station, or was pulled from the pages of a magazine or the stage of a strip club, each month a beautiful young woman earned the title. Since 2007, the monthly Miss Howard TV winners have ranged from college students to lingerie models and strippers.

Stern makes a point of interviewing each monthly winner on the program, starting with where they are from and what they do as a day job, then digressing into more personal topics such as boyfriends, lesbian experiences, sexual experiences, and so on. Yet, Stern remains polite and respectful of the women and compliments them on their beauty. And Artie Lange often chimes in with "This is the hottest chick we've ever had up here!"

The monthly honor of being Miss Howard TV includes bikini photos posted on the Howard Stern Web site, promotional activities, and the short segment telling viewers what is coming up on the channel for the month. Some of the women have gone on to modeling and other show business careers, including swimsuit model Joanna Krupa, who competed on *Dancing With The Stars*. Others have enjoyed their moment in the spotlight and returned to their day jobs with great stories to tell about their month-long experience as Miss Howard TV.

STERN, WOMEN, AND OBJECTIFICATION

Among the many protesters that have lined up to complain about Howard Stern are women's rights groups who claim that the show objectifies women. Does Howard Stern exploit women? Yes, but only women who enjoy being part of the craziness that is the world of Howard Stern. Many women's rights organizations make no bones about hating Howard Stern and have for years. They believe such exploitation of women tells men not to take women seriously and only to look at their bodies. Yet Stern has long defended the show, pointing out that the women who appear on the program all want to be there and enjoy showing off their bodies. The show gets numerous photos and letters from many women who want nothing more than to come on the show to promote their modeling or acting careers. Quivers, the one female on Stern's staff, takes the position of letting women do what they choose to do, and if they want to come on the show and disrobe, that's their choice.

In recent years, a more permissive society has led to fewer protests, and critics of Stern's treatment of female guests have had a hard time making headway when hundreds, if not thousands, of women try to get on *The Howard Stern Show* in bikinis, or less. Although many people still believe Stern exploits women, there is less commotion than in the past.

Although it does not minimize the issue of exploitation of women on HTV, those who know Stern off the air have often claimed that he is very respectful of the women in his life, whether his ex-wife Alison, Robin Quivers, his daughters, his second wife Beth, or his mom, all of whom he has been quite critical of on the air. He is, in fact, protective of the women in his life, in an effort to keep them away from the media circus. He has said that he would not be comfortable with his daughters following in the footsteps of some of his guests, but he would have to respect their choices as adults. This became an issue when his daughter Emily took the role of Madonna in a late 2005 play called *Kabbalah*, presented by the Jewish Theatre of New York. For the last ten minutes of what was described as an "ill-conceived" play, the role called for Emily to appear naked. Some stories say Stern was okay with the idea, and others say he begged her not to do it. Stern worried that she would get unwanted publicity and would have to deal with the wrath of his enemies. In the end, Emily quit the show after a few performances, also fearing that she would become an unintentional Internet star.[1]

FEMALE STERN FANS

Much to the surprise of many, there is a large female audience for *The Howard Stern Show*, in what has always been a male-dominated fan base. Some women have been featured on the show talking about how they love Howard Stern while their husbands do not; Gary Dell'Abate calls these "mixed marriages." The provocative interviews and freedom women on the show are afforded to talk about sexuality and express themselves are both welcome and fascinating to some women, while others are simply enamored with Stern or, in some cases, his cast or crew members.

Although Stern is not what most women consider "hot," he has an attraction much as a 1970s rocker in the day of the long-haired metal bands. He also has a great sense of humor, not to mention incredible success and wealth, which can make anyone, male or female, look sexier. Actresses, models, and female fans regularly tell Stern they adore him, especially porn actress Bree Olsen, who has told Stern that if he leaves Beth, she wants him. Stern is quick to point out that if he weren't rich and famous, most of these women wouldn't look twice at him. On the other hand, many women listen to the radio show simply because they find him funny.

THE NUMBER ONE WOMAN IN STERN'S LIFE: BETH

There has been one special woman in Howard Stern's life since 2000: Beth Ostrosky, now Beth Stern. Not unlike his relationship with Alison, Stern often talks on air about Beth and their life together. After nearly seven years together, the couple got engaged on Valentine's Day in 2007.

Stern had told the media, his radio and television audience, and anyone else who would listen that he had been soured on marriage after his divorce from Alison. He wavered about marriage with his buddy David Letterman on the *Late Show*. Letterman was also gun-shy about being married and for years stayed in a "living together" relationship with his girlfriend, plus his widely publicized office encounters. In time, and perhaps with the help of his therapist, Stern was able to get comfortable with the idea of marrying once again.

At this point in life, he knew that his preoccupation with his career was always a possible hindrance to a successful marriage. He has stated in several interviews that his radio show always comes first, though he knows this can get him in trouble in his relationships. It did with Alison and could with Beth as well. Through seven years together, Beth knew about Stern's dedication to his radio show and radio family and was not shaken by the possibility of having to share him with his radio family and his legion of fans. Beth also knew that she would be the topic of some of his program segments and that their life would be open to scrutiny, yet she stayed with him. As it turned out, Howard and Beth's personal life generated less airtime than his life with Alison. Perhaps the days of struggling to make it to the top were more interesting to listeners than the multimillion-dollar lifestyle of Howard and Beth. In addition, Stern did not have to talk about his relationship with Beth as the media was doing it for them. Gossip columns included frequent tidbits about their relationship, where they were seen dining, what they were doing, and so forth. Their public appearances and photos were splashed all over celebrity pages of newspapers, magazines, and Web sites as well as on television entertainment programs.

THE WEDDING

In October 2008, Howard Stern and Beth Ostrosky were married on a Friday night at one of New York's most exclusive restaurants, Le Cirque, a favorite of the couple. Under a 27-foot-high ceiling, the elegant main dining room of the world-renowned restaurant was a perfect setting for their star-studded wedding.

With the media perched outside trying desperately to catch a photo or grab some quick quotes from the guests as they made their way to and from the private affair, the wedding ceremony and reception took place in front of 180 of the couple's personal friends, celebrity friends, families, Stern's radio family, and Sirius executives. Unlike his first wedding, a quiet gathering in Massachusetts, news and photos of the wedding appeared everywhere.

Mark Consuelos, husband of popular talk show cohost Kelly Ripa, had become an ordained minister over the summer of 2008 and performed the ceremony for the couple in front of the 180 attendees. Among the notables in attendance were Jimmy Kimmel, Sarah Silverman, Joan Rivers, Barbara Walters, Chevy Chase, John Stamos, and Donald and Melania Trump. Billy Joel, a Long Island friend of Stern's, was also on hand, and sang for the couple at the reception.

Stern had material from the gala event to talk about on air for months to come, including the gifts they received, or lack of gifts, the behavior of his cast and crew, the X-rated Chevy Chase toast and more. The bachelor party that preceded the big event was also a topic for discussion. In contrast to what most people expected, Stern's bachelor party was subdued, quiet, and even dubbed "lame" by Stern staffers' standards. The reality was that the 54-year-old groom-to-be preferred a quiet time with 15 friends (mostly his coworkers), where they could drink, talk, and enjoy some great food at Nobu 57, one of Manhattan's most elite Japanese restaurants.

In a private room, the staffers, including Gary Dell'Abate and limo driver Ronnie Mund, toasted their leader on his impending nuptials, with no strippers and nothing particularly unusual. Stern was then presented with a giant cake in the shape of a microphone. Artie Lange had the best assessment of the evening, telling a *New York Post* reporter, "Never in my life did I think I'd be late for a bachelor party by arriving at 9 P.M.—or that I'd be drinking a Diet Coke."[2]

The ensuing on-air discussions included countless reviews of Ronnie Mund's drinking too much, acting inappropriately and essentially making a fool of himself. Artie Lange, meanwhile. noted on the air that he still could not believe that he was actually home from a bachelor party by 11.

All of this contrasted significantly with the infamous Fred Norris bachelor party several years earlier. The usually stoic Norris had had a bachelor party that drew far more attention than Stern's. Norris had gotten married while the show was on vacation, and none of the staffers knew about it until the vacation was over and they returned to the studio. Norris called Stern to break the news to him. Stern was quite shocked that his long-time friend would get married without him being present. Robin Quivers, who didn't even receive a phone call of the news, was angry at Norris for weeks. Nonetheless, when the shock wore off and the gang finally accepted that Fred Norris was now happily married, the guys decided to throw him a bachelor party. The party ended up with Norris, Stern, Dell'Abate, and other staffers in a Manhattan strip club where Norris drank, danced, and drank some more, until eventually he fell down, knocked himself out and ended up in a hospital bed the following day, completely unaware of the events of the night before . . . events that would be forever recalled on the Stern program. Yes, quiet Fred had the bachelor party that generated the most attention.

Some eight months after Stern's wedding, he returned to David Letterman's show, commenting that although Letterman could not make the event, Stern appreciated the generous $5,000 donation to a wildlife preserve (which Howard and Beth support) in honor of the couple. He then showed wedding photos and talked about how both star entertainers had taken the plunge into marriage after saying for so long that they wouldn't. (Letterman was married in a quiet, intimate service in March 2009.)

Letterman asked Stern if he planned to have more children, to which he replied that he had watched Letterman with his five-year-old son, and it seemed like too much work. It was pretty clear that with three grown daughters, Stern was not looking to expand on that.

HAS STERN MELLOWED?

Not unlike his early days on satellite radio, where many questioned whether Stern would lose his edge without ongoing FCC battles and quarrels with station managers, the same question was raised after Stern remarried. Once again, he remained undaunted by the lifestyle change when it came to his on-air personality. Although happy in his personal life with Beth, Stern's angst and frustration turned in a new direction: chess. A fan of the game since his teen years, Stern decided it was time to become a chess master. He became a regular participant in the Internet Chess Club and started taking online lessons from Dan Heisman a Philadelphia-based, U.S. Chess Federation National Master and author. Stern has brought chess up a number of times on the show, and his frustration at not being able to improve upon his game.

Recent years have also seen Stern spending more time in his unique interview mode with celebrity guests. Without having to worry about censoring his questions or their answers, he has taken more opportunities to delve into the personal secrets of those who are brave enough to sit with him in the studio.

The on-air discussion often returns to Stern's personal life, especially regarding Beth, whom he adores. Although he does discuss their personal and sex life, there is a sense that because Beth is a sweet, shy person who is not always comfortable in the public eye, Stern holds back out of respect and love for her.

CERTIFIABLY SWEET: MORE ABOUT BETH OSTROSKY

Either she's a brilliant actress playing a part or Beth Stern is indeed a true sweetheart. From all indications it's the latter. Before meeting Howard Stern, Beth Ostrosky never listened to *The Howard Stern Show*, and in fact, rarely listens to it today. She is the antithesis of many of Stern's no-holds-barred female guests. Beth is soft-spoken, shy, unpretentious, and just plain likable. She is humble and does not consider herself a celebrity, which is why she turned down an offer to be on the hit television show *Dancing With The Stars*.

"I'm not a celebrity," she told Pittsburgh TV talk show host Sally Wiggins who interviewed Beth before the couple was married. "What would I bill myself as, Howard Stern's girlfriend?"[3] she asked. Beth was a successful model who had appeared on the cover of *HSM* magazine several times, while writing an advice column for the now defunct publication. She had appeared in various other publications and had a best-selling calendar on the Internet, but after several years of swimsuit modeling, Beth wanted to put it all behind her and focus on her second greatest love (after Howard), helping and protecting animals. She not only hosted the 2008 *World's Ugliest Dog* competition for Animal Planet, but she is also a spokesperson for North Shore Animal League, an animal rescue center that rescues animals from all over the world and houses them until they are adopted. She also has plans to open her own no-kill state-of-the-art animal rescue facility in the Hamptons, on Long Island. During the days after Hurricane Katrina in 2005, Beth spent hours helping clean and nurse back to health numerous animals affected by the storm.

As for Stern, she claims that it was love at first sight. The two went out for coffee after the dinner party at which they met and saw each other the next day when he invited her over to watch a movie.

The Howard Stern Beth knows and describes is nothing like the Howard Stern the critics claim is vulgar and crass. He is the off-air Stern, compassionate, vulnerable, and, as Beth says, "a big sweet puppy dog, shy, self-conscious, embarrassed all the time . . ., that's the man I fell in love with."[4]

Beth is careful to steer clear of saying that what Howard Stern does on the air is an act, because she doesn't want to ruin his reputation, especially for those who hang on his every word. She keeps a distance from the Stern staffers, although she has become chummy with Lisa G., a Sirius newscaster and regular contributor to the Stern show. Beth's father, a big fan of Howard Stern before Beth met him, was concerned about his daughter dating the radio personality. Her mother was also less than pleased when she learned of her daughter's new celebrity love interest. "I told her and she slammed down the phone. We didn't talk for two weeks," said Beth in the interview with Sally Wiggins, explaining that the couple flew her parents to New York so they could all spend time together. Her parents soon grew to love the real, off-air Howard Stern, the one Beth adores. Beth also doesn't worry about the strippers and porn stars that come onto the show because, as she puts it, "he comes home to me every night."[5]

Stern may have lucked out in finding Beth. Now 37, Beth says she has never wanted to have children and wasn't even sure that she wanted to get married. She is, however, happy that she did. Being Mrs. Howard Stern has opened up many opportunities for her to promote her passion for saving animals, and she has become a celebrity of sorts.

MOVING FORWARD

Stern has hinted that when his five-year contract at Sirius-XM radio ends he will walk away and retire. He wants to spend more time with Beth and his daughters and wants to work on side projects. What those would be is anyone's guess. All those who know Stern are 99 percent sure retirement is not in his immediate future, although a new contract with Sirius could include more vacation time or fewer on-air days per week. Stern has more than enough money to enjoy retirement, but he has poured his heart and soul into his career for too long to leave. He is still having too much fun interviewing A-list celebrity guests, taking calls from his regular listeners, and being in the middle of the daily excitement that takes place in the Stern studio. Despite their occasional arguments, the chemistry between the cast and crew has never been better, and both the radio and televised versions of the program are running smoothly without FCC interference.

Now that the television channel affords Stern and his cohorts the opportunity to be creative with original programming, there are other television possibilities. Stern is always pondering new ideas, but the work involved in another book or movie seems to hold him back, as the radio show and HTV are full-time endeavors.

To keep the show fresh, Stern has gotten to know his audience very well over the years, fielding phone calls, looking at fan mail, and, with the help of Dell'Abate, taking the pulse of what his fans want. Perhaps it's simply part of being a good listener. It's also a large reason why Stern remains at the top of his industry. The way to stay successful in the entertainment field is to know what your fans want and to try to keep them coming back for more. Yet at the risk of overexposure beyond the daily radio shows and HTV, Stern does not venture very far into untested waters; he does not do appearances on other shows or cameos in movies just for the sake of it. At this stage in his career, he only does projects if he believes they will be well-received by his fans.

If and when Stern decides it's time to leave the business, he believes he will not be given his fair credit for all that he has done for the industry. Given that he has more than his fair share of critics and that he has outraged many conservatives, Stern might be correct about never receiving the honors due him. He might not win a Kennedy Center honor or other prestigious award, but someday a new breed of First Amendment challengers will recognize that Howard Stern opened many doors for their freedoms, much the way outspoken performers opened the door for Howard Stern and ground-breaking televisions programs like *All In The Family* or even *Laugh In*, decades earlier, opened up new avenues for television programs today. Still, Stern is far from modest about his own accomplishments, stating in a Charlie Rose interview: "The way people speak on TV, the way people do talk shows, the way people do sitcoms, the language . . . everything. I would even dare say that the reality television craze that we now see was brought on by this show. I probably am the single most important factor in modern entertainment today."[6]

Finally, Stern has demonstrated that in a world of constant hiring and firing, loyalty can still exist. While television shows have come and gone, and executives have bounced from job to job based on their most recent performance, Stern has kept his staffers with him for many years. The next chapter looks at the more recent activities of Robin Quivers, Gary Dell'Abate, Artie Lange, Fred Norris, and several of the other staff members who make up *The Howard Stern Show* as well as the Wack Packers.

NOTES

1. Bill Hoffman, "Stern's Daughter Cuts Smut," *New York Post*, January 5, 2006, http://www.nypost.com.

2. The Huffington Post Web site. "Howard Stern's Stripper-Free Bachelor Party," October 10, 2001, http://www.huffingtonpost.com/2008/10/01/howard-sterns-stripper-fr_n_130794.html.

3. Sally Wiggins, "Interview with Beth Ostrosky, Future Mrs. Howard Stern," October 2008 (Oct. 2008 is the posting, Interview was June 13, 2007), http://www.youtube.com/watch?v=VLMpZJsEGBQ.

4. Sally Wiggins, "Interview with Beth Ostrosky, Future Mrs. Howard Stern," October 2008, http://www.youtube.com/watch?v=VLMpZJsEGBQ.

5. Sally Wiggins, "Interview with Beth Ostrosky, Future Mrs. Howard Stern," October 2008, http://www.youtube.com/watch?v=VLMpZJsEGBQ.

6. Charlie Rose, "Interview with Howard Stern," March 27, 1997, http://www.charlierose.com/view/interview/5637.

Chapter 6

THE WORLD OF HOWARD STERN: THE RADIO (AND HTV) FAMILY

First it was Howard Stern, on his own at the microphone, awkward, nervous, and lacking in confidence. But he knew he had more to offer than just playing music, so over time he gradually worked a stream of consciousness style of radio, complete with comedy and listener phone calls, into his daily routine. In Washington, Fred Norris was asked to join Stern, and Robin Quivers was added as someone to bounce his creative ideas off of and to provide feedback, giving Stern more confidence. Then Gary Dell'Abate was added in New York City. Soon there was Jackie Martling, who was later replaced by Artie Lange. But there were more, so many more—crew members, writers, a limo driver, regular phone callers, more crew members for the television show, and a collection of unique characters of all shapes and sizes known as the Wack Packers.

By the time Stern joined Sirius Satellite Radio, the Stern radio family was quite extensive—and certainly more dysfunctional than most families. Web sites, discussion boards, blogs, and social media sites like Twitter and Facebook offer the many listeners an opportunity to keep tabs on the goings-on of this ever-expanding group. From the sites officially sanctioned by the *Howard Stern Show* to a host of Web sites created by fans, a subculture of Stern followers emerged dedicated, not only to Stern but also to the many people who make up his world.

Today, regular listeners and viewers of HTV are familiar with most of the Stern family. Like any family, there is plenty of fighting and many differing opinions, but there is also an undercurrent of loyalty and respect that keeps this large group working together with the same goal of providing top-notch, unique entertainment.

Much of Howard Stern's show has always been about reality. While Stern, Quivers, Norris, Dell'Abate, and Lange have essentially given us a fairly in-depth look into who they really are and what makes them tick, the extended family have also built their own followings.

Not unlike television, the personae of the Stern circle likely combine reality and exaggeration. After all, once the microphone and the cameras are on, people tend to exaggerate their actions, or at least show a side of who they are that they may not display every day.

Following is a look at some of Stern's extended radio family.

BENJY BRONK

In 1998, while in his late twenties, Bronk became a *Howard Stern Show* intern. He had spent several years kicking around from one odd job to another hoping to get into show business. In the course of doing the usual low-end tasks that make up the life of an intern, he began writing jokes and creating funny bits for the show. After several of his bits and ideas were used on the air, Bronk officially became a writer for the show in 2001.

In the ensuing years, his unassuming personality, plus his weight, has drawn the attention and typical attacks of his colleagues. At one point, Bronk won a Battle of the Blobs competition, losing more than 60 pounds, only to gain most of it back in the ensuing months. Bronk has been a good sport, participating in some of the raunchier Stern show games, such as Spin the Wheel of Benjy. In his underwear, with a cardboard pointer attached to his head, Benjy plays a human spinner, much like you would see on a game board. Typically, female contestants get to spin Bronk, who tries hard not to get dizzy. The results of the spins are usually activities that fall on the crude side. He has also participated in such activities as wrestling a Penthouse Pet. Anything for show business.

Despite participating in his share of amusing and demeaning situations, Bronk has contributed many of the humorous ideas over the years and has essentially replaced Jackie Martling as the on-show joke writer, with Artie Lange chiming in with his own comedy. Bronk is honored to be one of the elite few who regularly get to be in the studio during the show and occasionally voices an opinion when asked.

RALPH CIRELLA

Howard Stern's hair and wardrobe stylist, Cirella is a long-time friend of Stern and has been a frequent caller for years. He also designed the set in the Stern studios for the television audience on HTV.

Cirella is opinionated and somewhat arrogant, and he has a love-hate relationship with many Stern fans. The outspoken stylist has parlayed his frequent phone calls into numerous on-air appearances and even more Web pages in his honor. Cirella, who once finished at number four in his own AmIAnnoying.com list of ugly chicks, has made plenty of celebrity gossip columns while hobnobbing with the rich and famous and has even made his way into the famous Playboy mansion. As a result, he is a frequent judge on the Playboy evaluation shows in which Stern has two or three female guests who really want to be in the magazine. They face honest evaluations from a panel of judges, one of whom is often an actual Playboy photographer.

While members of the Stern radio family are known for being themselves, or at least having created extremely convincing characters, it's hard to tell if Cirella is putting on an act or just playing the role of antagonist whenever necessary. Either way, he does his part and contributes to the world of Howard Stern. Thanks to his loyalty, Stern keeps him around as his stylist even when he could really afford the best of the best.

RONNIE THE LIMO DRIVER

Ronnie Mund had been Stern's limo driver for more than a decade when Stern also made him his head of security. Somewhere along the way, Stern also started putting Ronnie Mund on the air. Perhaps Urbandictionary.com described Ronnie the Limo Driver best: "When he talks, you don't care about anything he has to say, when he is finished talking you just want your time back. Lacks all emotions except for anger."[1]

Voted the angriest person on *The Howard Stern Show* in the fall of 2008, Mund has a knack for making the wrong comment at the wrong time, cursing more than necessary, getting into petty fights with the staff (some real, some probably staged), and creating tension in and around the studio. He is an avid fan and patron of strip clubs and has been responsible for bringing many beautiful women to the show, several of which have won the honor of being the monthly Miss Howard

TV. As a result of his Brooklyn tough guy persona, Mund has taken his share of abuse from everyone associated with the show, laughing all the way to the bank.

JAMIE "JD" HARMEYER

If anyone seems in over his head while hanging with the Stern cast and crew, it's JD Harmeyer. The youngest of the prominent staffers, Harmeyer started as an intern in 2003. Shy, nerdy, but likable, Harmeyer has since become the show's media producer. Using several monitors, his job is to locate and pull audio or video clips for Stern to use on air. The clips are important aspects of the program, and Harmeyer has a knack for finding whatever is necessary. Being part of the Stern family means taking abuse and participating in on-air games like Strip Beer Pong, not to mention talking about his personal life. Nonetheless, Harmeyer is amenable to being included in the on-air activities, even if he fumbles his way through his answers and occasionally tends to sport a deer-in-the-headlights expression on camera.

SCOTT SALEM

Better known to many as Scott the Engineer, Salem has been with the show since the K-Rock days back in 1986, when Stern went into morning drive. Despite blaming him for anything that goes wrong in the studio, Stern considers Salem a top-notch engineer. Salem, however, always seems to have one foot out the door, ready to leave, and no longer take the Stern family abuse. However, working for the top radio show in the world is a very good opportunity and has given Salem, like many of the show staffers, notoriety he would never have otherwise enjoyed.

In more than a decade with the show, Salem is probably best known for taking part in a bet that he could not do 17 push-ups. Being overweight and a smoker, he wasn't thought to be in very good physical shape, prompting the challenge from Stern, with significant money involved. Like many of the other games and activities on the show over the years, the Push-up Challenge became a big event, complete with a referee, and pop singer Debbie Gibson called in to sing the national anthem. In the end, Salem did the 17 push-ups, but, as is so typical of Stern show events, controversy reared its ugly head as the claim was made by other staffers that he didn't do 17 *legitimate* push-ups. Salem's ensuing tirade became legendary. In the end, the videotape proved that he had indeed met the requirement, and he eventually walked away with the money.

Salem was also featured as the announcer covering the Bowling Beauties tournament, a four-part original series on HTV in which 16 bikini-clad women competed for top honors. Much to everyone's surprise, he took the job very seriously and broadcast the competition as if viewers were watching a legitimate Professional Bowlers Association tournament.

MIKE GANGE

Another show staffer who started as an intern, Mike Gange has risen to the position of supervising producer of HTV. The lofty title notwithstanding, he has a lot of responsibility but still caters to Stern and the cast, who love to give him a hard time.

Although Gary Dell'Abate handles the all-important production duties for the radio show, which spill over to the television programs as well, Gange takes care of what is uniquely necessary for the visual appeal of HTV. Like Scott Salem the engineer, Gange is frequently blamed for whatever goes wrong.

One of the few single male staffers on the program, Gange is usually interested in the female guests and seems to magically appear in the hallways outside the studio when the new monthly Miss Howard TV is going into the studio for an interview. At one point he got into an on-air war of words with Artie Lange while vying for the attention of one of the Bowling Beauties. Gange does not take part in the show's games and challenges as he is focused on making sure the production value remains top notch, but he is probably best known for his former out-of-studio relationship with porn star Kendra Jade Rossi.

RICHARD CHRISTY

Like several of the other Howard Stern regulars, Richard Christy was a fan and contributor to the show before becoming part of it. Christy sent song parodies and left messages on Gary Dell'Abate's answering machine, some of which were funny enough to make it on air.

When the infamous "Stuttering John" Melendez left *The Howard Stern Show* in 2004, they held a contest to win John's job. The winner would be selected from participants who showed off their talents throughout the course of a week. Christy, a heavy-metal drummer with an offbeat sense of humor, won the contest and has been part of the show ever since, contributing comedy ideas, comedy bits, and lewd behavior.

Along with Sal the Stockbroker, Christy has become one of the bad boys of what is already a pretty bizarre group. It's become fairly well established that Christy, along with Sal, will do just about anything for a laugh. Prank calls featuring an array of character voices, unusual stunts, and weird games, such as two-on-two nude basketball (in which he lost to two women) are all part of the saga of Christy, who still plays heavy metal. Christy has also hosted original programs for HTV, including one in which he interviews aging porn stars, in a mock version of the sophisticated program *Inside the Actor's Studio*.

SAL THE STOCKBROKER

Sal Governale, a former stockbroker, began making prank calls to Gary Dell'Abate back in the mid-1990s and was eventually hired by the Stern show in 2004 after he finished second to Richard Christy in the Get John's Job contest.

His job title has yet to be defined, but Sal has made a name for himself from his pranks, his warped logic, and the bizarre antics he performs with Christy. A stand-up comic and one of the Killers of Comedy (a group of Stern staffers and Wack Pack members who have toured doing mostly offensive comedy material), his racist humor has both offended and amused audiences, although he claims he's not really a racist.

Sal is often confused and does not understand how his words and actions are considered inappropriate. His jokes about Beth, for example, resulted in his being the only staff member to be banned from Howard and Beth's wedding. The jury is out on whether Sal is as dumb as he appears or if it is all just an act. There have been some curious moments, such as when Howard 100 News told a story about him that he deemed to be false, he kept demanding that they give a "traction" (meaning a retraction), much to the amusement of everyone in the studio.

Sal's pranks and the uncensored on-air stunts with Christy give the show an added edgy, unpredictable quality, often stretching the boundaries of good taste—which in the world of Howard Stern is truly an accomplishment. In some ways, Sal and Christy are akin to court jesters whose goal is to make the King of All Media laugh. If they can amuse Stern, they will keep their jobs, because they are also keeping Stern's many fans happy.

An interesting note on Sal is that he claims his dad was addicted to the lottery. As he has explained on the air, his dad would buy hundreds and thousands of lottery tickets, so many in fact that he would need other people to fill them out. With the dream of winning the millions of dollars that was usually up for grabs in the New York State lottery, Sal's father would sink a large portion of his earnings into the lottery every week. According to Sal, his dad actually won a smaller prize of $30,000. What did he do with the money? He spent most of it on more lottery tickets.

LISA G.

Lisa Glasberg, or Lisa G., the petite on-air news reporter for Howard Stern's Sirius radio show, primarily reports the news taking place in the world of Howard Stern. Glasberg also has a life outside of the Stern family, making her a fringe member of the group.

Glasberg started in radio by playing a major role in the success of the hit New York City radio show featuring Dr. Dre and Ed Lover, and she has since worked as a correspondent for CBS-TV, WOR, E!, and Real TV while also being featured in the *New York Times*, and GQ, where she was named one of the most Eligible Women in America. Lisa G. also runs her own public relations business.

Despite hosting some parties for the gang and being the only other woman besides Quivers to be part of the daily shows, Glasberg takes her fair share of abuse from the guys. Her straitlaced, businesslike demeanor has led to her being questioned about her love life and her sex life. The interplay when she is in the studio is often that of the little sister in the male-dominated Stern radio family. She is frequently teased and riled, but Stern plays the role of the big brother who watches out for her. She's also sharp and tries to hold her own during personal inquiries and general abuse, especially from Mund. She occasionally gets the better of her tormentors. A seasoned broadcaster, Lisa G. always seems to be a step away from having her own program. She even suggested a cooking program where she would cook with the Wack Packers, though it never materialized

WACK PACKERS

Over the years more than 50 people have been designated as part of the Howard Stern Wack Pack, a group that has gained notoriety for being an odd collection of misfits and unique characters. The Wack

Packers range from a racist clown to a comic reverend to individuals with very specific abilities or disabilities. Names like Junior the Farter, Stuttering John, Jeff the Drunk, and Crackhead Bob convey the general idea of what makes the Wack Packers distinctive. Others, such as Gary the Retard, are indeed disabled but enjoy their moments of fame and notoriety. Some Wack Packers make a rare appearance on the program to judge a contest or take part in some on-air activity, others phone in periodically, and a few have been featured on some of the original HTV programs. Following are a few of the most popular members of the infamous Wack Pack.

Andrea Brooke Ownbey

Back in 2002, Andrea became the first Miss Howard Stern, a title she has held ever since. During the show's on-location broadcasts from Las Vegas, the 19-year-old exotic dancer won the distinction of being the world's dumbest stripper, getting six of eight very simple questions wrong. Her baby voice, IQ of 88, and good looks made her a perfect Miss Howard Stern, especially because Artie Lange and others could make jokes about her while she was present that would go right over her head.

The problem with Ownbey was her self-destructive persona. Excessive drinking, volatile behavior, too much plastic surgery, and a lack of direction in life drew concern from the Stern cast and crew, while also making her the perfect subject for a reality TV show. The HTV show, called the *Andrea Ownbey Reality Show* which had a few carefully edited episodes, included drunkenness, confrontations with friends and family, more drunkenness, partying, and even more drunkenness.

Ownbey's appearances on *The Howard Stern Show* eventually became more infrequent. Her initial cute and playful behavior lost some of its charm as she continued on her self-destructive course, often appearing totally inebriated on air. In 2009, Ownbey was in a terrible automobile crash in which she hit a telephone pole and was thrown from the car, fracturing her skull. Given less than a 10 percent chance of survival, doctors operated on her for some six hours. As of the writing of this book, she is recuperating.

Daniel Carver

Wack Packer Daniel Carver is a the former leader of the racist Ku Klux Klan, the infamous organization determined to "protect the rights of white Americans" through the use of violence, threats, and even the murder of people of color or other minorities. The hate group originated in the south and became known for wearing white sheets and burning crosses on the lawns of African Americans, Jews, or anyone else who did not support their beliefs.

Stern and company need add only occasional comments when Carver begins a tirade, and they mostly let him figuratively hang himself with his own hateful and bigoted remarks. Stern has used Carver in offbeat games such as Hollyweird Squares, and he even did a comedy roast of Carver with African American, gay, Jewish, Hispanic, and lesbian comics providing the jokes. Carver dismissed the comics with his usual offensive retorts, although he may not have understood the humor of their jokes or the underlying messages. At one time, Carver did movie reviews for the show using a rating system of one to four burning crosses. Stern has also used Carver as the resident bigot to provide narrow-minded opinions.

Beetlejuice (Lester Green)

Lester Green, known on the show as Beetlejuice or the Juice, is a mentally challenged dwarf with a high-pitched voice. He drinks often and has played the role of judge in a number of Stern show contests and has even landed an original program on HTV. He is one of the best-known members of the Wack Pack. He makes public appearances with some of the Killers of Comedy, does voice-over work, and has landed parts in feature films such as *Bubble Boy* and *Scary Movie 2*. With music provided by Richard Christy, Green's original Beetlejuice song has been played on *The Howard Stern Show*.

Yucko the Clown

Yucko the Clown achieved attention and eventually became part of the Wack Pack by running onto the field during a major league baseball game while carrying a Howard Stern sign. Sporting the traditional clown outfit and makeup, Yucko is an angry, nasty clown spewing a never-ending rant filled with insults and curses. Being part of the Stern show has helped Roger Black, the man behind the world's meanest clown, build his audience. Away from the Wack Pack, Yucko has his own following and has appeared on MTV's Stankervision and Jimmy Kimmel's talk show. He also has a Web site from which he sells his own DVDs.

ROLE OF THE WACK PACKERS

These are just a few of the many Wack Packers who are part of the world of Howard Stern. Many others have also had their on-air moments and have gained a following away from the show. Stern has long defended the Wack Packers, claiming he is not trying to make fun of or humiliate Wack Packers such as Gary the Retard, Beetlejuice, or Eric the Midget. Stern, Lange, and Dell'Abate all see most of the Wack Pack as people who do not have a lot going on in life because of their disabilities or, in some cases, the paths they have taken, including drinking or drug abuse. *The Howard Stern Show* has given them some degree of celebrity status and, in most cases, the opportunity to make fairly significant money by being themselves.

Stern, Dell'Abate, and the cast and crew are very cautious not to exploit the Wack Packers. They carefully determine what activities the Wack Packers take part in and when they should appear on the show. They also stay in touch with those who help care for some of these people to make sure they are not unhappy with their roles on the show. Artie Lange was once quoted in an interview, "I genuinely think that the people that come on our show enjoy it, they enjoy the attention, and I think it enriches their lives that would have been really boring, mundane and, for lack of a better word, horrible without this love."[2]

THE WORK ENVIRONMENT

The constant interactions and arguments among cast, crew, the Wack Packers, and regular callers provide an ongoing soap opera sub-plot for fans to follow while also making for entertaining on-air conversation. Whether it's a discussion of what to do about Artie Lange walking off the show, falling asleep during the show, or getting into a near fist fight with his assistant Ted, or Ronnie Mund getting angry at newscaster Lisa G. over interfering in his personal business, or Sal not being invited to Howard and Beth's wedding after constantly making jokes about Beth in his stand-up act, there is always something to talk about. Petty arguments, claims of unfair treatment, miscommunication, and so much more are typical of any family and are often played to the hilt on the show.

The Stern staffers, however, work hard to filter numerous ideas to Gary Dell'Abate and Stern for games, bits, pranks, guest activities, and so on. It is not an environment in which one can be thin-skinned, however, because some ideas click and others are shot down. The anxiety of being creative in such a fast-paced environment can get to staffers, and tempers occasionally flare, creating more fuel for the show. Numerous arguments have made their way into the studio, some real and some staged. Often it is Gary Dell'Abate's job to discuss what the conflict is and who is upset. Stern prides himself on being the voice of reason, but he often lets the on-air combatants battle it out. The characters working within the world of Howard Stern are so well known that callers will sometimes take sides and get involved in the in-staff fighting. Those who cannot get through to the program will respond on the many fan-based Web sites or e-mail the show.

Despite their disagreements, the turnover rate at *The Howard Stern Show* is minimal, far less than at most creative programming, where burnout and disputes send people packing on a frequent basis. The success of the program has been so huge that nobody can be accused of bringing the show down, and Stern is very loyal to those who have helped make the show so successful.

Andy Richter, Conan O'Brien's long-time right-hand man, once commented, "You know how these shows work, one person gets a job and then they bring in all of their friends." [3] While Rosie O'Donnell (*The Rosie O'Donnell Show 1996-2001*) and many other performers were guilty of doing just that, Stern staffed his show with people who got the gist of what he was doing and proved their worth. It was after showing their dedication to the show that long-lasting friendships emerged . . . which explains why Stern has outlasted so many comedy radio or television programs and has maintained such a massive fan base. Although even Stern has commented on air and in interviews that sometimes he is loyal to a fault.

THE INNER CIRCLE

Artie Lange

From terrestrial radio to Sirius Satellite Radio, Artie Lange has continued to supply the show with his sharp, often acerbic, quick wit, while still being both vulnerable and honest about his own tumultuous life. Somehow, while making the rounds as a very successful stand-up comedian and being on the show almost every morning, Lange found time to write the book *Too Fat to Fish*, an autobiographical account of his ups and downs on route to the Stern show. The book came out in late 2008 and became an instant best seller. Lange provides an honest account of his many personal struggles complete with plenty of profane yet comical moments, many of which stem from his own self-deprecating humor. The book includes the famous pig incident, familiar to long-time Stern fans, in which Lange, for an episode of *MADtv*, in a pig costume for a spoof of the film *Babe* and the TV series *Baywatch*, sat in his car snorting cocaine until he was caught and subsequently fired from *MADtv*.

The love-hate relation between Lange and himself has often taken center stage on the Stern Show. On one side, Lange is proud to be pulling in major amounts of money as a top headline performer, but on the other side he walks a fine line trying to maintain his weight, which has ballooned up to more than 300 pounds, and his sobriety and has spent time in a rehab facility. Stern, the staffers, and the fans are all rooting for Lange to make it without the need for heroin or any other drugs.

Lange, who released his own comedy CD *Jack and Coke* in late 2009, is not only a major sports fan (Yankees and Giants in particular) but is always ready to take on a sports challenge as well. At one point during the show's weeklong visit to Vegas, Lange went one-on-one in a basketball game with a top female player and dominated during the early part of the game. However, as the game progressed his stamina faded fast. He lost the game but dazzled Stern fans with some excellent outside shooting.

More recently, while promoting his book and comedy shows, Lange made an infamous appearance on the first episode of *Joe Buck Live*, a sports talk show on HBO. Lange seemed like the perfect guest to stir things up a little, which is exactly what he did. Pulling no punches, he let loose with a no-holds-barred, profanity-laced comedic barrage that drew laughs from the studio audience but mixed reactions from Stern listeners the next day on the air, not to mention the press. While some argued that Lange wasn't funny, including sportscaster Mad Dog Russo, the real question wasn't about the humor but about whether or not the profanity was inappropriate. Lange argued that such language is allowable on HBO. The Joe Buck camp and supporters argued that it was not appropriate on that program. Lange has since been banned from HBO, at least for the time being.

What is most appealing about Artie Lange, and what makes him the ideal cohort for the show, is that he is honest and straightforward, especially about himself and what goes on in his life. The truth is, despite what he says on or off stage for laughs, Lange has a heart of gold and is genuinely appreciative of being part of the Stern family. He respects and admires Stern and considers Stern's approval very important.

Robin Quivers

Robin Quivers, meanwhile, often provides the one shred of logic in some of the more illogical arguments that take place in the world of Howard Stern. It's very rare that Quivers loses her cool, although years ago she was almost always angry about something. Quivers has mellowed during her years as part of the Stern show.

Despite being part of the most reality-laced show on radio and television, Quivers maintains some secrecy about her private life. When she bared her soul in her autobiography, *Quivers: A Life*, it was the first time many of the listeners and even some of the staffers learned very much about her life, especially about her abusive childhood. On the show, Quivers is never completely straightforward when discussing her relationships, which included several years with a Mr. X. She also dated comic Jim Florentine, which generated plenty of grief from her co-workers, and more recently had a younger boyfriend named Mark.

In 2006, Stern gave Quivers a Mercedes convertible in appreciation of all of her hard work and loyalty for so many years. She also took to race car driving. In 2007, she entered the Toyota Pro Celebrity Race along with Martina Navratilova, Kelly Hu, George Lucas, Aisha Tyler, and others. Although she did not win, she did finish the race. According to the racing Web site raceschool.com, "Robin had a little taste of cement today and hopefully, she didn't like it. Not a big hit, more of a 'brush' coming out of Turn 3. She has a good feel for the track and just has to push herself a bit to get that speed up."[4] Quivers also generated attention from the gang when she bought a boat, which had everyone vying for a chance to ride on it or drive it.

Gary Dell'Abate

Gary Dell'Abate, also known as BaBa Booey, spends much of his limited free time with his family. At the station, he remains in control, freeing up Stern and company to do what they do best because they know they are in good hands. A radio producer needs to organize all aspects of the daily show. The more segments in the daily broadcast, the more work for the producer. Because *The Howard Stern Show* is more than just taking phone calls, like much of talk radio, and isn't about playing music, Dell'Abate has his hands full. He books celebrity guests, and because celebrities have very tight schedules, this can be a juggling act.

Then there are the thousands of people who want to promote themselves, their Web sites, and/or their businesses on the show—or just want to come on the show and participate in a contest or simply get naked. Dell'Abate needs to sift through the cards, letters, e-mails, and phone messages from thousands people with help from the show's interns.

Is it any wonder that Dell'Abate has limited free time? He does make some celebrity appearances, and being a big New York Mets fan, he got to throw out the first pitch before a game at CitiField, the Mets' new ballpark. Plenty of reporters were on hand, and Dell'Abate was written up on sports pages because the pitch was so far from the catcher that the umpire standing way off to the side caught it. As one blogger posted on the SportsUnderground.com Web site, on May 11, 2009, "It quite possibly is one of the very worst [pitches] of all time."

Along with handling the daily wrap-up shows, which are broadcast on HTV, Dell'Abate also organizes and hosts *The Friday Show*, a compilation of bits from previous programs that are used when Stern is not on the air.

The popular Stern Show music trivia game Stump the Booey has been a long-time fan favorite, but Dell'Abate has also used his music trivia background to win VH1 music game shows, and he has appeared on *Hollywood Squares* several times. He's been happily married for more than 25 years, and one of his neighbors says he is a terrific dad and great all-around person to know, always friendly to his neighbors and very involved with his kids.

Fred Norris

Fred Norris, meanwhile, continues to maintain a low profile on and off the program and is not often seen doing promotional activities. Yet Norris is not as quiet as one would guess and is often on stage fronting his rock band, King Fred, in which he plays lead guitar and sings. King Fred has appeared with Motorhead, Quiet Riot, Eddie Money, Patti Smith, the Foo Fighters, Green Day, Kid Rock, Rage Against the Machine, Offspring and at Ozzy Osbourne's annual Ozzfest.

The motorcycle-riding Norris is more cerebral than most of the gang, as he has demonstrated time and time again by showing off his knowledge (or at least his penchant for trivia), winning the game Win Fred's Money time and time again.

Over the years, Norris has been a sound engineer, writer, producer, impressionist, and announcer and has taken on almost any role necessary. He is often turned to for his opinions and typically has an analytical, insightful approach. Whether anyone agrees with him or not, he always sounds like he knows what he's talking about. Despite once almost getting into a fist fight with Stuttering John Melendez over an in-studio love scene being played between Melendez and Norris's wife Alison, Norris is usually one of the last ones to lose his cool, which can be difficult in such a high pressure environment.

ADDITIONAL ACTIVITIES

The celebrity status of most everyone associated with *The Howard Stern Show* has resulted in offers for public appearances and other activities. Attaching the Stern name to an activity or local event in any manner can be very beneficial. With this in mind, businesses try hard to draw Stern staffers to grand openings or to make appearances at their clubs, restaurants, and stores. As a result, the Stern staffers try to be selective when it comes to endorsements. As for their own projects, the link to Howard Stern has built a greater following for Norris's band, while enhancing Artie Lange's already strong fan base and making Robin Quivers a celebrity in her own right. For Sal and Richard (Sal the Stockbroker and Richard Christy), who have taken to doing shows together, it has allowed them to build their comedy careers far more easily than they could have without the link to the show.

REGULAR GUESTS

While they are typically looking to promote their latest show, appearance, book, CD, or other project, Stern's regular guests are generally those who most comfortably fit into the show's approach and the overall insanity that is the world of Howard Stern. Most are confident enough in their careers and public image that they are not scared to reveal something about themselves on the show. They are outspoken, frank, honest, funny, and genuine when talking with Stern.

Some frequent guests are A-list celebrities, but Stern guests also include unusual comics, B- and C-list actors, and doctors. For example, Dr. Sal Calabro—a plastic surgeon who has worked his magic on some of Stern's guests and gives his medical opinions on breast implants and other topics—is a frequently called guest. Other regulars include angry insult comedian Lisa Lampanelli; the always bizarre Sharon and Ozzy Osbourne; brilliant comedian Gilbert Gottfried; eccentric former NBA star Dennis Rodman; and real estate billionaire and host of *Celebrity Apprentice* Donald Trump; not to mention several porn stars, including Bree Olsen and Ginger Lynn.

Many other noncelebrity guests have used their Howard Stern appearances to enjoy their 15 minutes of fame. On the other hand, that 15 minutes of fame can backfire. For example, a Connecticut teacher named Marie once appeared on the show in a hottest wife, ugliest husband contest. The school was not happy that she appeared on the Stern show in her bikini and that she violated the morality clause in her contract, but even more significantly, they were not happy that she lied about being sick and missed a day of work to appear on the show. She was pressured to resign and subsequently sued the school board.[5]

Stern and his legion of fans have played a role in other firings, such as that of *New York Post* writer John Mainelli. After Stern's first year on satellite radio, Mainelli started reporting that Stern's ratings were not very good and that he might be returning to terrestrial radio. Stern made it clear on air that Mainelli was running a radio consulting service, which is in conflict with the impartiality of his radio reporting. As a result, Mainelli was fired from the *New York Post*. Mainelli blamed Stern and his staff for the firing and had plenty of choice words for them in his response.[6]

LOVE 'EM OR HATE 'EM

Over the years, it has become very apparent which celebrities Howard Stern likes and which he detests. He has a penchant for comics because he does comedy for a living. Stern has always liked comics who are upfront and honest, as opposed to those who hide behind characters or simply aren't very funny. For example, although he had good things to say about Chris Rock and invited comics like Gilbert Gottfried and the late Rodney Dangerfield to appear on the show often, he never had anything nice to say about Rosie O'Donnell, whom he did not find funny. Though after trashing her for many years, he surprisingly had her on the program in 2009.

Don Imus and Rush Limbaugh are easy targets for Stern who disagrees with their viewpoints and has a general disdain for both outspoken radio personalities. Stern has been very critical of other stars, such as Oprah Winfrey, for whom he believes there is a double standard. Stern even led an offensive, asking people to write to the FCC in response to a sexually inappropriate show Winfrey did in 2004, noting that he would have been fined in a minute, but she got off without a scratch. He has also expressed his anger over the fact that she has a satellite radio channel and can't be bothered to appear on it herself, while he works hard to give his audience something to listen to. He has also taken aim at stars, such as Kirstie Alley, who he believes are peddling nonsense. Stern contends that an overweight star should not be promoting a weight loss program. Although some of his mocking is all in fun, such as that of his friend Joan Rivers, whom he claims kept her career going for years by harping on her ex-husband's suicide, his disdain for other celebrities is quite genuine.

As is the case with the general public, celebrities' responses to Stern also vary widely from the many return guests who enjoy taking part in the show to those who don't like what he does. In an interview with Charlie Rose, Stern responded to a question about whether he will ever be recognized by his peers. "I'm so despised and so envied. Don Hewitt and Bill Cosby—and other people who are power brokers in the industry—discount what I am. Even in their defense of me against the FCC, they all say one thing. They all say they hate my show and they hate me, and they say I have no talent. But they defend my right to free speech. That's how history books will remember me. I am Tiger Woods, Mickey Mantle, and JFK all rolled into one. But I never will be given the credit," replied Stern.[7]

In May of 2008, country singer and actress Dolly Parton threatened Stern with a lawsuit stemming from a comic bit where Stern's sound engineers mix up vocal comments of a celebrity to say something other than his or her actual comments. This type of comic editing is commonly used by radio DJs and TV comedy shows for comic effect, but Parton didn't think the routine was funny as it made her sound as if she had made racist comments.

"I have never been so shocked, hurt, and humiliated in all my life," the star of 9 to 5 said to reporters. "I cannot believe what Howard Stern has done to me. In a blue million years, I would never have such vulgar things come out of my mouth. They have done editing or some sort of trickery to make this horrible, horrible thing," she added, apologizing to her fans and saying that she was completely devastated.[8] As of the writing of this book, the lawsuit has not yet materialized.

TONS OF FANS

And finally, there are the fans, without whom none of Stern's success would have been possible. Stern fans range from casual occasional listeners to a very devoted, sometimes fanatical group who will prank call CNN and other media outlets in honor of their hero. Before the Internet, Stern's most dedicated fans had to take their chances writing, faxing, or calling the show in hopes of having a letter read or actually being heard on air. This is still part of the ritual of the most faithful Stern fans, but the Internet has opened up an opportunity for numerous fan sites and chat rooms for sharing all sorts of facts, trivia, discussions, and debates about Stern, Robin Quivers, Artie Lange, Fred Norris, Gary Dell'Abate, the Wack Pack, and everyone else involved. Following the saga of the cast, crew, and assorted misfits, including other fans, is a full-time hobby for some.

Calling and getting through to the show today is no easy task. Regular callers have the inside track with their familiar antics, and newcomers need to be even more clever in hopes of getting through. Fans willing to bare their souls, and sometimes their bodies, can occasionally get onto one of the in-studio games, but it means being selected from numerous entries.

Although many fans are content listening to the King of All Media on Sirius radio programs and watching HTV, some are determined to get up close and personal, bordering on stalking the star. In 1998, one such fan, Dan Wagner, wrote a book called *Getting to Howard: The Odyssey of an Obsessed Howard Stern Fan* (Ilicium Books). Like everything else surrounding Howard Stern, the book was met by rave reviews from some and hated by others who considered Wagner to be nothing but a crazed stalker.

Whether one perceives Wagner as a fan, a stalker, or both, he does take readers through his own journey, which began with his incessantly faxing the show and continued to his meeting crew members and Wack Packers. He even concocted an Emmy Award scam to present Stern with such a trophy and meet his idol. Unlike the books by Stern, Quivers, and Lange, Wagner's book was far from a best seller, but it did provide a look into the mind of one Howard Stern fanatic.

And then there's Doc, a chiropractor by trade, who recalls the day Howard Stern went on the air in October 1999 and, as Doc puts it "shocked his audience by revealing that he was getting divorced from his wife of 21 years of marriage and the mother of his three daughters." Doc, a pseudonym for a man who would become one of the most exuberant of obsessed Stern fans, claims that day's program remains the most compelling radio he has ever heard.

Doc went from being a casual fan, who discovered the world of Howard Stern in the late 1990s, to being obsessed. At first, he taped every show and listened to them all in their entirety. Soon he decided he needed something more—interaction with the show. After reading Wagner's book, he decided to start writing to the show, not just to Stern but to Gary Dell'Abate, Fred Norris, and Robin Quivers. He sent

gifts for Dell'Abate's sons and Stern's daughters. In need of some vali-
dation from his hero, he sent a letter claiming to be his wife complaining about her husband's obsession and how it was destroying their
marriage. Could Stern just send something to his sons—a photo or anything from the show, he begged, under the pretense of a frustrated
spouse.

In March 2000, after sending numerous letters and items to the program, Doc and his family got the thrill of their lifetime when Stern
read the so-called wife's letter on the air. Shortly thereafter, Stern sent
two signed photos to Doc's boys. Arguably, the greatest Stern fan of all
time, Doc went to great lengths to amass an autograph and photo collection of anyone and everyone who was connected to the show in any
manner. Doc went on to create the ultimate Howard Stern shrine,
which grew to include more than 100 autographs that he kept in a separate room behind his office, away from patients but accessible to true
Stern aficionados as invited by Doc. At one point a TV entertainment
news show wanted to do a segment on the ultimate tribute to Howard
Stern and film the shrine.

Doc is very likely the leading collector of Stern-related autographs,
and he says he's considering putting his collection into a book someday
if he can obtain copyrights for the many photos he has collected.[9] Sure,
there are many other fans with great stories of Stern obsessive behavior
to tell, but Doc epitomizes their true love of, and fascination with,
their hero.

IT'S A MAD, MAD, MAD, MAD WORLD

The world of Howard Stern is aptly described as "mad," and there is
always plenty going on both inside and outside the studio. As indicated
in the animated opening of his HTV programs, Howard Stern is very
much the ringleader of this nonstop circus, in the center of it all, maintaining peace and order in the midst of chaos. And he's also at the center of the chaos.

Although fans of the new breed of radio personalities proclaim Stern
to be past his prime, Stern listeners disagree, finding that the ongoing
saga and endless string of top-name guests and absurd on-air antics still
rule all of radio, terrestrial or satellite. The subscriber base for Sirius
and HTV has continued to grow, proving that Howard Stern and company are obviously still doing something right in their uniquely dysfunctional radio family.

NOTES

1. Urban Dictionary Web site. "Ronnie the limo driver," http://www.urbandictionary.com/define.php?term=ronnie the limo driver.

2. Internet Move Database web site. Artie Lange biography. http://us.imdb.com/name/nm0005119/bio.

3. Andy Richter, personal interview, 1999.

4. Danny McKeever, "Press Day—April 3," 2007, http://www.raceschool.com/raceblog/leading-up-to-race-day.html.

5. Daniel Schwartz, "As American as Apple Pie: 'Hottest Wife' Teacher Sues School Board for Due Process Claim." Connecticut Employment Law blog, July 2, 2008, http://www.ctemploymentlaw-blog.com/tags/marie-jarry/.

6. Orbitcast.com Web site, "Stern Gets John Mainelli Fired," September 22, 2006, http://www.orbitcast.com/archives/stern-gets-john-mainelli-fired.html.

7. Charlie Rose, "Interview with Howard Stern," March 27, 1997, http://www.charlierose.com/view/interview/5637.

8. Fox News Web site. "Dolly Parton Threatens to Sue 'Howard Stern' Over Fake Sound Bites," May 15, 2008. http://www.foxnews.com/story/0,2933,355884,00.html.

9. Personal interview with Doc. May 2009, by the author.

CONCLUSION: THE CONTRIBUTIONS OF HOWARD STERN

ENJOYING HIS LIFE AND HIS SUCCESS

What has Howard Stern achieved besides great fame and fortune? Through the years, Stern has been the focus of debates between censors and those fighting for freedom of speech, between liberals and conservatives, between fans and critics, and even between politicians of different viewpoints. Stern has used his stature to redefine the FCC guidelines repeatedly, support or denounce politicians, rile celebrities, build careers, infuriate or gratify sponsors, get a law passed in New York, and change the face of radio.

His style of reality radio has likely had some influence on reality television, and he has played a major role in making it permissible to talk about once taboo topics on the air. In his world, surrounded by friends, admirers, misfits, and celebrities he remains in the cocoon that is radio, one person behind a microphone, from which he can speak his mind freely and in his own way affect culture and society. Stern has made people take notice of what he has to say, and whether listeners agree or disagree, they are hearing a point of view that may not often be expressed by others in the media for fear of censorship or recrimination or simply because it is not politically correct.

Stern has helped move the media toward greater open-mindedness by pushing the boundaries of freedom of speech. He has sometimes pushed too far, but bold steps can often achieve a little ground in the pursuit of greater freedoms.

Nonetheless, Howard Stern will always be remembered as a shock jock, a label he hates because he does not find it appropriate. Stern does not do what he does primarily to shock people, but he is doing what he honestly finds to be entertaining. This has also set him apart from his competitors who are largely trying to draw the public's outrage and shock.

THE MANY SIDES OF HOWARD STERN

Stern has also proven that he can lead a very different life on and off the air, day in and day out. Actors play roles, but Stern simply plays different aspects of who he is as a person. Although he is genuine in both capacities, the Jekyll and Hyde approach to life allows him to be the edgy performer and vent behind the microphone, while being himself, a kinder, gentler Howard Stern and a good husband, father, and son off the air.

As for Stern himself, the road has been rockier than he leads one to believe. He has, over the years, had many self-doubts about himself and his career and was even suicidal at times. He struggled through a painful divorce from someone who was his rock early on in his career. He questioned whether or not he was a good father who was there enough for his daughters, sought therapy, and often battled with his own insecurities. Yet when he is in front of a microphone he is the king. Today, with Beth in his life, Stern appears to be very content. Unlike Lenny Bruce and others who fought long and hard to make a difference and champion freedom of speech, Howard Stern has come out rather unscathed from the many battles and has been able to enjoy his life and his success.

FURTHER READING

Quivers, Robin. 1995. *Quivers: A Life*. New York: HarperCollins.

Stern, Howard. 1993. *Private Parts*. New York: Simon & Schuster (for mature readers).

Stern, Howard. 1995. *Miss America*. New York: HarperCollins (for mature readers).

Wagner, Dan 1998. *Getting to Howard: The Odyssey of an Obsessed Howard Stern Fan*. Ilicium Books (for mature readers).

Website: Howardstern.com (for a mature audience).

INDEX

About the Author

RICH MINTZER, a long-time Howard Stern fan, is the author of more than 50 nonfiction books on a wide range of topics. In 1983, he worked as a producer and writer at WNBC radio while Stern was also at the station. Mintzer has written about entertainment as a reporter for both the *Hollywood Reporter* and *Variety*. He currently lives in Westchester, New York, with his wife and their two teenagers, Rebecca and Eric.